Live Your Nonsense

Marie-Louise von Franz, Honorary Patron

**Studies in Jungian Psychology
by Jungian Analysts**

Daryl Sharp, General Editor

LIVE YOUR NONSENSE

Halfway to Dawn with Eros

A Jungian Perspective
On Individuation

DARYL SHARP

For my late friend of some fifty years, the Canadian sculptor Jerry Pethick, whose nonsense and Eros knew no bounds. See pages 98-103.

Library and Archives Canada Cataloguing in Publication

Sharp, Daryl, 1936-
    Live your nonsense : halfway to dawn with eros / Daryl Sharp.
(Studies in Jungian psychology by Jungian analysts ; 129)

Includes bibliographical references and index.

ISBN 978-1-894574-31-0
1.   Sharp, Daryl, 1936 – Relations with women. 2. Man-woman relationships – Psychological aspects. 3. Jungian psychology. 4. Psychoanalysts—Biography.
I.   Title. II. Series: Studies in Jungian psychology by Jungian analysts ; 129.

BF175.S4916 2010   150.19'54092   C2010-901601-7

INNER CITY BOOKS
Box 1271, Station Q, Toronto, ON M4T 2P4, Canada.
Telephone (416) 927-0355 / Fax (416) 924-1814
Toll-free (Canada and U.S.): Tel. 1-888-927-0355 / Fax 1-888-924-1814
Web site: www.innercitybooks.net / E-mail: booksales@innercitybooks.net
Honorary Patron: Marie-Louise von Franz.
Publisher and General Editor: Daryl Sharp.
Senior Editor: Victoria B. Cowan.
Office Manager: Scott Milligen.

INNER CITY BOOKS was founded in 1980 to promote the understanding and practical application of the work of C. G. Jung.

Cover Image: "Spectrum" (Teddy-Bear Rules), wall piece by Jerry Pethick,1986; mixed media on glass. One element of a triptych.

Printed and bound in Canada by Thistle Printing Ltd.

CONTENTS

See final pages for other Inner City titles

Where love reigns, there is no will to power,
And where the will to power is paramount, love
is lacking. The one is the shadow of the other.
—C.G. Jung, CW 7.

What the mate of a writer finds hard to understand
is that a writer is working when staring at the wall.
—Prof. Adam Brillig.

Wrtiting is no trouble: you just jot down ideas as they occur
to you. The jotting is simplicity itself—
it is the occurring which is difficult.
—Stephen Leacock.

I shall live badly if I do not write,
and I shall write badly if I do not live.
—Françoise Sagan.

If you ask me what I came to do in this world,
I, an artist, I will answer you: I am here to live out loud.
—Emile Zola.

Introduction

It is pretty well known by now that I am enamored of Carl Jung, that my *raison d'etre* for the past forty years has been to promote the understanding and practical application of his work. I have been a faithful acolyte explicating Jung's work as best I can with whimsy and good humor, focused more on Eros than Logos. I am not an Edward F. Edinger or Marie-Louise von Franz, but editing and publishing some of their books makes me feel close to them.

It was the love of Jung's work that propelled me out of a juicy mainstream career into a new life some fifty years ago. The major manifestation of my new life, other than my four accomplished offspring, is the canon of works I have published, including some I wrote myself. I would like to be remembered, if at all, for my devotion to the monumental task of rediscovering oneself. This marks me, in the language of philosophy, as an essentialist rather than an existentialist. I am obliged to my colleague J. Gary Sparks for succinctly noting the difference:

> Our being guided to develop into a whole person or a unitary personality . . . implies that the person we are becoming was there from the beginning; otherwise, where does the knowledge of who we are meant to be come from? We are forced to conclude that the basic pattern of wholeness that is unfolding was there *in potential* from day one.
>
> Indeed, Jung is not an "existentialist" but rather an "essentialist." The existentialist says that we create ourselves. The essentialist says that we discover ourselves. The existentialist says that "existence precedes essence," which means that we are first born and then we create who we are—our essence—out of the choices that we make. The essentialist position says that "essence precedes existence," which means that we are already born who we are and the process of identity creation is discovering what is already there.[1]

*

---

[1] Sparks, *At the Heart of Matter: Synchronicity and Jung's Spiritual Testament,* pp. 125f.

A man's soul is initially in rags, if not actually ragged. A man may flounder for many years without a soul, making do with a charming and competent persona that pays the bills and gets him ahead in his profession. I mean no blame by saying this. It is how the Western world works. We like to think that love makes the world go round, but at any moment, downsizing or a medical disaster or a financial collapse can stop it in its tracks. It is simply the dark side of the capitalist system, which erupts every once in a while. Women may feel bereft, but men are often the most hard hit, for they are the traditional breadwinners and they hurt at a soul level. (I may address this in a later book but meanwhile I am pressed to write about Eros rather than capitalism or the stock market.)

It takes many encounters with women, sexual or otherwise, for a man to get a handle on his inner woman, his soul. But it is an imperative if a man is to grow up. This involves differentiating his ideal of a mate from the real women he becomes involved with. This is not easy, and not generally accomplished without dialoging with a relatively objective professional therapist. I favor those who are Jungian-oriented, but more important than a school of thought is the empathy between the two parties.

I am by nature introverted and chary of self-revelation, and so the impulse to write this book initially went quite against my grain. However, my reluctance was overcome by dismay at the extent to which current books on or about Jung and analytical psychology have focused predominately on Logos values—intellectual dissertations and/or discourses unpacking his ideas and extrapolating on them—or, often, claiming to better them. I am really troubled by this trend.

Now, I too am a child of the Enlightenment. I valued my initial education in maths and physics. But I have to ask, why wasn't I taught what all that was missing? Simple answer: my instructors were taught to make me as single minded as they were. Not their fault; it was the culture at the time, the 1950s, and the Heisenberg Uncertainty Principle—much less Eros—had not yet penetrated into university curricula. Alas, I was able to receive a Bachelor of Science degree with hardly any exposure to the humanities. It was only by happenstance and dogged determination that I went on to correct this lacuna by a postgraduate education in literature and philosophy. And since then, my interest in Eros has escalated far beyond anything I ever learned in university.

As well, I recently had a dream, halfway to dawn, inviting me to step out of the shadows, an open-ended injunction hard to ignore.

Still, it was not easy to know what to write in these pages. In the end, this book is anecdotal and mostly about the various relationships I have had and from which I have learned who I am. The accounts are not chronological. Some are early on, some later. All life is such a mix, and it is also true that I can't always tell fact from fiction. But what is real here is tone and feeling.

The subtitle of this book, "Halfway to Dawn," refers partly to the writing of it in the wee hours. It also implies a glimmer of consciousness on the horizon, not that I am any the wiser. We all exist *in potentia,* and what comes to fruition is more or less out of our hands, though not beyond our ken if we put our mind to it.

*

I am not a sage or a preacher on high. I am not an expert on nonsense and of course I don't know what it is for anyone else. You may not even notice your nonsense, or, if you do, you might file it in a generic folder or drawer labeled peccadilloes or bullshit. (In Ireland it's known as gobshite.) Not my concern. So by default—as they say in the world of digital technology, where for arcane reasons ones and zeros rule the roost—the best I can do is recount some of my own and others' nonsense and say what I see at its root, psychologically. That is the content of this book. Novices beware; this is not the deep end, but it could waft you there.

The point I would like to make is that nonsense is not necessarily frivolous, foolish or sinful. It may be politically or socially incorrect, but it is often a pointer to the essence of one's personality, which is what we Jungians call individuation—becoming who you were meant to be. There is no denying that this is an elusive, subjective concept, not something that can be imposed, or judged, from outside. Yet we have an intellectual history of learning from the experience of others, which is why I write and publish books and you read some of them.

There are some rather sexually explicit scenes and language in this book. Well, no surprise; that is life and nothing to apologize for. Indeed, it is rather unavoidable when referring to the many ways in which masculine and feminine may be embodied and what lies behind their coupling or inhibits it.

It is worth noting that nonsense doesn't always involve Eros, and the erotic is not always nonsense. But in my experience the two have generally gone hand in hand, and I can live with that.

*

The title of each vignette here does not relate much, if at all, to its content. On the whole, the entries are not substantial enough to be called chapters, but I just didn't want to leave them naked, so I plucked phrases at random from that vast interior storehouse that is the unconscious, much as artists of any genre often do in naming their works. Sorry, I may be obscure, but I don't claim to be wise.

Nor, indeed, have I ever aspired to walk in the footsteps of Jung, who ever so discreetly never published a word about his close personal relationships. And the recent publication of his autobiographical *Red Book* leaves me quite ambivalent. It is of course an important historical document that will be appreciatively perused by committed Jungians, but I fear that mean-spirited critics will not treat it kindly, and that the general public will be baffled.

*

Overall, this book of nonsense is simply a riff on my experience and understanding of myself—not unlike the masters of cool jazz who have lightened many a dark night for me: Miles Davis, Paul Desmond, Chet Baker, Stan Getz, Gerry Mulligan, Dizzy Gillespie, Wes Montgomery, Hans Koller, Charlie Parker, and on and on.

I am pleased and proud to have lit some candles of my own over the years. This book is somewhat more personal than my others, but *what is left to us at an advanced age except not to dissemble?*

On the whole, in the grand scheme of things, I am in the dark as much as anyone. I grapple with personal demons just as much as my clients do. Being a Jungian analyst doesn't make one immune to life's travails, only, possibly, more aware of them—but of course I have my blind spots, which we call complexes, that obscure my understanding of myself. Perhaps, when you come right down to it, we are all "ghost whisperers."

This evening I watched the film *Coco Chanel,* starring Shirley Mac-Laine. It is beautiful in many ways, especially in all the nonsense Chanel lived on her own terms, come hell or high water. She had some difficult patches, but always stuck to her guns and gut-instinct. She was a heroine for all time. I do love spirited women, but more of that later.

*

It recently came to my attention that I really don't like or understand rap or hip-hop. This undoubtedly means I'm behind the times, but I can't help that. As a beloved mentor once said to me, "I can live with dying, but I'd rather not be ill for long." In the end, his wish was granted. Here is my tribute to him, for what it's worth in the Beyond:

> Raise no memorial stone. Although we miss
> him, let the rose bloom every year for him.
> He's Orpheus, and his metamorphosis
> Is everywhere. We needn't scan the rim
>
> Of forests for more names. Once and for all
> It's Orpheus when there's song. He comes and goes.
> And isn't it a marvelous windfall
> When he stays a few days longer than a rose?
> For you to know him he must disappear!
> Though he was terrified of vanishing
> And while his word transcends his being here,
> he's gone already where you cannot go.
> His hands are not ensnared in lyre string
> And he obeys, stepping beyond us now.[2]

I write for my own generation, as do most writers. Younger readers will, rightly, take from it what suits them. We must all live our own non-

---

2 Rilke, *Rainer Maria Rilke, Sonnets to Orpheus,* sonnet 5, "Raise No Memorial Stone."

sense. We automatically become older, but not necessarily wiser or more psychologically alert. I have been practicing for forty years, but I am still a novice in terms of dealing with the distressed psyche, including my own.

> If I give my heart to you tonight,
> will you still be by my side.
> Or will you be gone, with the morning sun;
> Like a restless bird in fly.
>
> Take me in your arms,
> and let the love you see,
> Wash away your sorrows.
> Let the morning be ours too keep.
>
> and if I should tell you of a love that I had,
> will you still be there for me.
> or will you away to a faded love,
> searching for freedom's game.
>
> Take me in your arms,
> and let the love you see,
> wash away your sorrows.
> Let the morning be ours to keep.
>
> If I give my heart to you tonight,
> will you still be by my side.
> or will you be gone,
> with the morning sun.
> Like a bird who yearns to fly.[3]

So saying, I aim only to give you some whimsical food for thought, and perhaps license to live your own nonsense, for it may contain the truth of who you really are.

*****

---

[3] "Listen to Your Heart," Eva Cassidy, on *No Boundaries;* Ascap.

One
Whiskers on a Frog

If there is one thing I know for sure, it is that that I am unconscious most of the time. Not always, but mostly—and, moreover, usually unaware of it. That is in the nature of the psyche: the ego cannot see itself from the outside.[4] This means that everything is colored by subjectivity, from experiments with electrons to the belief, or not, in God.

Of course, this results in nonsense of all sorts, much of it not my personal (ego) doing but instigated by what in my profession we call the shadow. This is an elusive concept covering all manner of moods and activities that regularly upset a sedate, ego-centered, persona life—rage, tax fraud, illicit liaisons, cheating at cards or golf, you name it. Still, I have to accept responsibility for what my shadow does. That is an ethical imperative; no way to escape it short of jumping off a bridge.

Case in point: the current (December, 2009) fracas over Tiger Woods' infidelities. I have every sympathy for the man and his family. The potentially positive outcome is that the masses will realize that we all have a shadow side, and acting it out has consequences. This could lead more people into analysis, and I think the world might be better off for that.

What is nonsense, anyway? Is it simply, by definition, something that makes no sense? Well, if it were that simple, I could let myself off the hook and wouldn't have to write a book about it. But I'm already in too deep to scarper. And it's not all bad. Listen to Jung:

> I have seen more than one case who got stuck in too much wisdom and was unable to live, and what is the use of wisdom when it stands in the way of life? The young want to learn whatever there is to learn, and then go out into life and experience more. People sometimes think that analysis

---

[4] Jung teaches that the unconscious, via the Self, is the "Archimedean point" that sees the ego objectively in dreams and such. This is advanced psychological thinking, and we're not yet there in this book or century; perhaps later or never.

will take the place of life, they protect themselves in that way against much nonsense that might be lived. But mind you, *if you don't live your nonsense you will never have lived at all,* and the meaning of life is surely that it is lived, not avoided.[5]

Live your nonsense! Jeez, what an evocative remark. I have been reeling ever since I came across it.

Again, the point is, nonsense is not always frivolous. It is often *of the essence* in the evolution and manifestation of one's personality. Better said: Not all nonsense is frivolous, nor is all frivolity nonsense. It all depends on one's *attitude.* This is far, and only the swift reach it and are delighted.[6]

And what is personality? Well, in the Jungian scheme of things, personality evolves through the progressive, conscious awareness of ego, persona, shadow, anima/animus, together with a working relationship with the Self, the organizing principle and center of the overall psyche (comprised of consciousness and the unconscious). And the goal is not to become a better person but to understand who you are, warts and all. It is not an easy journey, and those lost along the way are legion.

Midlife is like when you're halfway through reading one of those lengthy bestselling thrillers (Ludlum, Grisham, Clancy, etc.); you've lost sight of the plot and hardly remember the players, but you keep on going just to see what happens next. Of course, there are those who lose all heart and snuff out their own candles, and this is especially tragic for those left behind, wondering what they might have done to make a difference. I have wept for more than one such.

****

---

[5] *Visions: Notes of the Seminar Given in 1930-1934,* p. 1147 (emphasis added).

[6] I thought that clever last sentence just came to me out of the blue, but it turns out to be an example of cryptomnesia (see my *Jung Uncorked,* Book Three, pp. 16ff). I suddenly recalled that Nietzsche said it first: "Thinking of oneself gives little happiness. If, however, one feels much happiness in this, it is because at bottom one is not thinking of oneself but of one's ideal. This is far, and only the swift reach it and are delighted." (Notes, 1875, in Walter Kaufmann, ed. and trans., *The Portable Nietzsche,* p. 50). Neither my use of it nor Nietzsche's makes much sense, but that is in the nature of nonsense.

Two
The Walrus Laments

I woke up to another rainy day. I was recently separated from a long-term partner (let's call her Veronica) who decided to reinvent herself with a new man. It was hurtful; we were together for twenty-two years. I knew she had met and loved a fellow artist, and we had lived with her ambivalence for some months. Still, it was a shock when on the brink of bedding her one day she said to me, "I can't do this anymore." Only then did I realize that her feeling for her new love was not whimsical but deep seated and an essential move on her path to individuation.

Back to the beginning: my fate with Veronica was sealed on the evening we danced at a Jungian auction event. She was so sultry and after Zurich I was hungry for that. I fell into her the next day and never looked back. We were lovers for many years, though we never lived together.

I might have tried harder to keep her with me, but being a proponent, personally and professionally, of going where one's energy wants to go, I could not begrudge her decision. And after flailing about I finally didn't impede her leaving and we parted amicably. For all I knew, it was best for both of us. I tend to live in the present and accept what is. And we still have in common our astrophysicist daughter Jessy Kate (aka JK, who wowed me at the age of twenty by having the alchemical Axiom of Maria tattooed on her shoulder, in Greek).

The man Veronica left me for and later married said to me at their reception, "I admire you for letting her go."

I replied, "No, it wasn't like that. She just went away, following her heart and her energy. I had to respect that. I didn't like it much, but it wasn't my call. Congratulations, be happy."

Anyway, for some time I was feeling alternately bereft and fancy free; glad to live alone but often lonely. In this state I fell back into nonsense and musicland. How about these haunting lyrics written by Hoagy Carmichael in 1939 and popularized by many singers since:

I get along without you very well
Of course, I do
Except when soft rains fall
And drip from leaves
Then I recall
The thrill of being sheltered in your arms
Of course, I do

But I get along without you very well
I've forgotten you just like I should
Of course, I have
Except to hear your name
Or someone's laugh that is the same
But I've forgotten you just like I should

What a guy
What a fool am I
To think my breaking heart
Could kid the moon
What's in store
Should I fall once more
No, it's best that I stick to my tune
I get along without you very well
Of course, I do

Except perhaps in spring
But I should never think of spring
For that would surely break my heart in two
What's in store
Should I fall once more
No, it's best that I stick to my tune
I get along without you very well
Of course, I do

Except perhaps in spring
But I should never think of spring
For that would surely break my heart in two.[7]

---

[7] "I get along without you," by Nina Simone, on *Love Songs,* 2005; Ascap.

And then Marissa crossed my path.

She was a winsome middle-aged brunette with flashing green eyes and a handsome cleavage. She said on the phone that she'd read all my books and wanted to get to know me better. She sounded altogether like the kind of woman I tend to fall in love with, that is, a wounded bird. No wonder *La Bohème* is my favorite opera. Whenever I watch it, I want to leap on the stage and save Mimi. We call it a savior complex.

I took this lovely lady to lunch at the local Thai restaurant, where we sifted through her projections onto me and a few I was developing onto her. It was very pleasant and hands-off.

I walked her back to my house and her car. "Marissa, it's nap time for me," I said.

"Alone?" she smiled.

I hesitated. I had recently made a pact with myself not to get involved with attached women with undifferentiated complexes. As well, I was dating her analyst, more or less. You can bet I had a few conflicts running side by side.

"You'd better go," I grimaced.

Marissa responded by jumping into my arms and licking my ear.

"I like you!" she said. "I want you!"

Bold talk! Jeez, M was so pretty and enthusiastic and smelled like flowers, so I let instinct take over.

"Come in," I said, "I'll show you around."

I said it as a spur-of-the-moment courtesy, but well aware that it was an indefensible indiscretion. More, I don't often show visitors my inner sanctum.

M trotted happily through my three-story Victorian house, admired the paintings, the books and the swimming pool, and finally spread herself out in the master bedroom, clothes provocatively loosened.

I was intrigued and inclined to take it all as a fantasy, but when I lay beside her she made it real. To be honest, I am in general rather easily seduced. However, in this instance there was quite a bit at stake, so I did try to resist the rising tide, but Marissa's mercurial modesty simply overwhelmed me. I am not an anchorite.

"That was super swell," she said after. "I reckon I could love you," nibbling my nose.

"Yes, me too," I said, for she had expertly plucked my strings. "But you already have a mate."

"A technicality," said M. "There's nothing there anymore."

My mind was awhirl with the sensational lovemaking and what it portended. But I was cautious, by nature a puer, a post-adolescent who likes to keep his options open.

"Let's talk tomorrow," I said.

But tomorrow never came for me and M, for the very next day she told her analyst, my sometime paramour, all about our frolic, and the latter was so deeply hurt that she told M she'd better skedadle back to her husband in Broken Elbow, Saskatchewan, which M dutifully did, without so much as a fare-thee-well to me. And so, for a momentary pleasure I definitively lost my putative lover, whose rage overcame her usual capacity for forgiveness.

Well, I learned from that what an idjit I was. Not all my fault, but a lot. Nonsense, for sure. But possibly another rung on the ladder to wholeness. Who's to know in the moment? I didn't have a dream to guide me either way, only her earrings left behind on my bedside table.

This morning I woke up with a bruised wrist—red, black and blue. Those frigging aliens won't leave me in peace. A fractured ankle and two broken metatarsals in three years. And now the wrist. What next?

It isn't all fun and games being an idjit; sometimes you really have to work at it.

****

Three
Never Ever Land

Now, this is a really hard account to write, but a joy too, for it takes me back to my callow youth, to when I first arrived in London, England, flat broke, after spending my meager savings entertaining and making love with a Parisienne multilinguist in a Left-Bank hotel with mirrors on all four walls and ceiling. Monique was a cute and very sexy young lady. We met at a dance hall on the *Champs d'Elysées*. I took her home in a cab and at her door she said she wasn't allowed to have visitors. I grimaced. She touched my hand. "May I stay with you?" she asked shyly.

Well, what could I do? As any true gentleman would, I took her in and fed her. She improved my French and we enjoyed each other, but she abandoned me as soon as I ran out of Traveler's checks, which took about four months.

Well, not for me to put the blame on Mame, boys; I just didn't see it coming. I was twenty-two at the time, starry eyed and just off the boat at Le Havre. I had no street smarts at all. I was a happy-go-lucky lapsed Procter & Gamble junior executive, hardly wet behind the ears, so it qualifies as juvenilia. This is not to say I regret that episode in my life; on the contrary, I'd like to repeat it. But of course that's unlikely, much as I'd like to emulate Maurice Chevalier, who at my current age reportedly had three paramours, not counting Audrey Hepburn and his *femme de ménage* (cleaning lady).

Downhearted and crestfallen at Monique's defection, I took the train and ferry across the pond to England. In London I quickly found a room in Earl's Court, where most newcomers in those days got a foothold on life in the Big City. My digs weren't much, but better than a cave or a tent in Hyde Park.

I was extremely excited, over the moon, to be in London. I began to feel like a grown-up as I walked the streets zealously seeking work. Within a few days I had talked my way into a low-level job at the posh department store Harrod's in Knightsbridge. Somehow, the fact that I had a degree in journalism qualified me to work in a back room packing books. I didn't mind. Two pounds a day was enough to live on in those days, and the boredom was relieved by making out with young lady clerks on the roof during coffee breaks. I mean, we were all so age-appropriately horny. You understand, this was a time when I had no concept of Eros, much less what was entailed in having a relationship.

When I wasn't working I went to Covent Garden, to ballets and operas, concerts and theater. It was all new to me, and so thrilling I could hardly sleep. I was fresh from the cultural desert that was then Toronto, and found myself in an oasis that was incalculably seductive.

At the same time I fell among companions of a like mind, ex-patriot Canadians who were wannabe writers, sculptors, painters, actors (Rick Jones, Donald Sutherland), all of that. You couldn't cross the street without bumping into a poet. And in the pubs we frequented, the pretty lasses with an eye to the future were not reticent with their favors. Becoming Canadian by marrying one was all the rage in those days, and for all I know it still is.

****

Four
Fearless Fosdick

"I like my women soft and my likker hard."

That remark is attributed to Jack Kerouac, the original "bad boy" of the 1950s' so-called beat generation. The acerbic gnome Truman Capote said of Kerouac's bestseller *On the Road,* "That's not writing, that's typing."[8]

And so perhaps it was, but his typing sold millions, while mine lan-

---

[8] See Jon Winokur, *W.O.W.: Writers on Writing,* p. 85. This is a delightful little book of candid remarks, from the profound to the pompous, by well-known authors, their complexes writ large; required reading for any writer or wannabe.

guished. Kerouac: "Fuck structure and grab your characters by the time balls"[9] —Whatever that means . . .

Arrggh! I thought I had more to say than Kerouac, but nobody was listening. I think now that's how it should be—let an artist spend his or her twenties and thirties, even forties, learning their craft, and then burst onto the cultural scene like a Mondrian or F. Scott Fitzgerald. What I had to say as a youth wasn't worth saying, it was just juvenilia. Nevertheless, I came to think of myself as a struggling writer, which had a glamorous, Byronic ring about it and gave me a sustainable persona among my peers, who were not all as talentless as myself.

And then, soon enough, wouldn't you know it, I fell in love and the merry-go-round abruptly stopped.

Damn! Falling in love disturbed me no end, and not just because the woman in question (let's call her Beatrice, why not; Dante did) was my roommate Daniel's girlfriend at the time. We accidentally made love one weekend while he was away, and I was immediately lost, transported even. I knew right away that she was my fate. (Daniel was very gracious about the turn of events, and when we married he was my Best Man.)

A few days later I checked out of my menial job at Harrod's and made my way to the south of France, to a youth hostel in the small town of Sète on the Mediterranean coast. Beatrice had been there the year before, and the plan was for me to hole up for a couple of months until she could join me. (She had a cockamamie job as a substitute teacher in secondary modern schools.)

Well, this youth hostel in Sète was something very special. It had a mère and père aub (mother and father of the *auberge)* who were tolerant and empathetic. They welcomed me and my typewriter to a tent on the side of the hill above the lodge. During the day I read Rilke and Kafka and Nietzsche and other modern European writers, or typed my heart out trying to emulate them. At dusk I strolled down to the port and helped the fishermen unload their catch. I spent the evenings writing passionate love letters by hand and eating my liver. I was so lonely for Beatrice, she had me by the balls.

---

[9] Ibid., p. 57.

Correction: my feeling for her had me bolloxed. She didn't have a lot to do with it, except to be at a distance. I stewed with love, steeped in sentimental nonsense. I knew nothing at that time of the psychological concept of projection; knew not that it was all in my head. There were opportunities with other women but I eschewed them all. I mean, I stayed celibate because I was smitten. All was dross that was not Beatrice. I would have waited for her forever, like Penelope for Odysseus; I wove fantasies during the day and tore them out at night. The Four Freshmen, and many others, sang it like this:

> There is no greater love
> Than what I feel for you
> No greater love,
> No heart so true
> There is no greater thrill
> Than what you bring to me
> No sweeter song
> Than what you sing to me.
> You're the sweetest thing
> I have ever known
> And to think that you are mine alone.
> There is no greater love
> In all the world, it's true
> No greater love
> Than what I feel for you.[10]

Well, B finally arrived and put me out of my misery. More: she came on a little motorbike, a brand new Lambretta. We had a joysome reunion and after a few days making love in the tent we set off to tour Europe on her bike. This was a huge lot of fun, though we crashed more than once. We always stayed overnight in youth hostels, which cost next to nothing and were better than motels: comfortable beds and everything in the kitchen to cook for yourself. It was a remarkable time for us both, and I could not get enough of Beatrice. We were wildly, passionately attached. We coupled often, whimsically, anywhere and everywhere—on hillsides,

---

[10] "There Is No Greater Love," lyrics by Marty Symes and Isham Jones; Ascap.

under bridges, in trees, in lakes and in the ocean, under tables, once in a Venetian gazebo, twice in chapels, once in a belltower, on and on, enjoying life like a romantic comedy. I believe our first son was conceived in the Adriatic. Perhaps there is no greater nonsense than what lovers get up to. The very memory of it leaves me agape.

To me, B was a powerful woman, not intellectually but emotionally. She was not ambitious but she was adamantly free spirited. She had lost her parents at an early age and was a wounded bird, prone to moods; one day loving and frolicsome, the next day brutally standoffish. Talk about eggshells; I was always on edge, but I just loved her all the more. I wanted to marry, to own her, but B would have none of that nonsense. Well, until she became pregnant; then she agreed.

What folly! I gained a wife and lost a lover. I think she resented being grounded, cornered, and thereafter grieved to be free. We went on to live together for twelve years and have three children. But I never fulfilled her expectations of what a mate should be—and my expectations of her, I now believe and it pains me to say, dulled her potential for a more creative life of her own. She was a terrific mother but not cut out to be a wife. I think I was an adequate father, but not meant to be a husband.

I adored B; she was a goddess to me, but she could not carry that weight, nor could I of a father/god. After we moved back to Ontario in 1969, to live in the house she'd inherited, I became progressively more despondent and crazed. I was late to the North American hippy scene but I embraced it with unstinting enthusiasm. I cultivated marijuana (Belltower Fineglow) behind the corn, hosted pot parties and was known to dance naked on tables in the garden. I often took refuge in the basement, toking and writing or playing at being a photographer. I felt unloved and was slowly dying.

It was 1971. I was then director of a group called the Playwrights Co-Op, publishing plays. My first extramarital affair was with my secretary, Anna, half my age and cuter than a button. We had a few hash brownies and went to experience the Rolling Stones at Maple Leaf Gardens. We fell into her bed after, still giggling.

I had a few other flings, but all disastrously short-lived because I felt indissolubly wed to B, umbilically attached, as it were, and no other woman touched my heart as she could.

In desperation, on my knees, I went into Jungian analysis. B rejected talk therapy and put her faith in astrology. My analysis and her tracking of the stars just drove a bigger wedge between us.

All this is of course in retrospect. We were too young and unconscious to know what was happening between us or talk frankly about it. The world had been our oyster; in time it became our sting-ray. Or to use a musical metaphor, we slip-slided from major to minor.

B was not an outstanding beauty, no Betty Grable or Lana Turner or Angelina Jolie. She never wore makeup. She was simply hauntingly attractive, soft, ethereal, charismatically evincing veiled passion. I was enchanted. I could never get enough of her physically, but emotionally I could not penetrate her quicksilver, beguiling, ever-changing persona. I had once engaged her gypsy soul, but after we married she never gave herself to me. She simply consented to be loved, and hammered me the next day because I wasn't a handyman. I tried endlessly to please her, but it was never enough. Over time that broke my spirit, and perhaps hers too. I was emotionally dependent on her but insensitive to her personal plight. I do not judge B as harshly as I take myself to task for disappointing her. She was my fate, alright, but it almost killed me. On the other hand, it was an experience I desperately needed in order to grow up.

Of all the men I know or have worked with analytically, none is or was more of a puer (mother-bound) than me. And of all the women I've known, B took the cake for animus possession. And with me being anima-possessed, we really didn't stand a chance. You could say that her animus trumped my romantic, wounded-bird anima; no argument from me. We did go for couple counseling, but after two sessions listening to her scolding me for being myself, I would have no more of it.

Anyway, I have long since stopped parsing our problems, which were, I now believe, psychologically intractable.

The literal capper to our slowly decaying relationship manifested the day I attempted to remove a bee's nest hanging under one of the eves. I was stung, more than once. I had an immediate anaphilactic reaction—

swollen tongue, difficulty breathing, shivers, rash and fever. I fell off the ladder, comatose. An ambulance was called. I spent the next two days in the hospital and the next year going for weekly allergy tests. It turned out that I was allergic only to my wife, the queen B . . . Call it psychosomatic/oedipal (Freudian/medical) or symbolic/synchronistic (Jungian/meaningful coincidence). I don't know for sure, but naturally I favor the latter.

Okay, maybe she was allergic to me too. I only know that she didn't want to make love with me, and that was my bottom line.

After a few more months of simmering animosity, victims of our mutual unconsciousness and defeated by the complex nonsense that regularly bedevils relationships, we separated. I left my three young children. I missed them all terribly, and B too, for the four years I was away. But that's another story, much too raw for these pages.

Anyway, strange as it seems, when I returned to Toronto from Zurich, B assumed I was coming back to her. Well, I had a better idea of who I was by then, and it didn't include living with her. What we had together was an important rung on the ladder of my life. It wasn't all nonsense, but I no longer had a desire to sort wheat from chaff. She did not take kindly to my attitude, and stalled the formal divorce for another five years. In retrospect, I might have treated her more kindly and come to love her again, but I just wasn't there. And she couldn't make head nor tail of who I had become. In 1983, on the very day of our formal divorce, I bought the house in which I have lived and worked ever since.

*

I had to go back fifty years in my head to write the above, so there are plenty of gaps. Of course I could fill them with more nonsense, but I am mindful of not abusing our childrens' memories of their late mother, or indeed of me. So let's take a break—lock and load:

> Well, it's hard to be a gambler
> Bettin' on the number
> That changes ev'ry time
> Well, you think you're gonna win
> Think she's givin' in

A stranger's all you find
Yeah, it's hard to figure out
What she's all about
That she's a woman through and through
She's a complicated lady, so color my baby moody blue,

Oh, Moody blue
Tell me am I getting' through
I keep hangin' on
Try to learn the song
But I never do

Oh, Moody blue,
Tell me who I'm talkin' to
You're like the night and day
And it's hard to say
Which one is you.

Well, when Monday comes she's Tuesday,
When Tuesday comes she's Wednesday,
Into another day again
Her personality unwinds
Just like a ball of twine
On a spool that never ends
Just when I think I know her well
Her emotions reveal,
She's not the person that
I thought I knew
She's a complicated lady, so color my baby moody blue,

Oh, Moody blue
Tell me am I getting' through
I keep hangin' on
Try to learn the song
But I never do.[11]

As Jung notes so succinctly:

---

[11] "Moody Blue," lyrics by Mark James and Elvis Presley; Ascap.

When animus and anima meet, the animus draws his sword of power and the anima ejects her poison of illusion and seduction. The outcome need not always be negative, since the two are equally likely to fall in love.[12]

B was my fate at the beginning, for sure, but it was also my fate to leave her. I loved her intensely, obsessively. This song by Cat Stevens, before he morphed himself into Yusuf-Muslim and out of the mainstream, says it all:

> Now maybe you're right and maybe you're wrong
> But I ain't gonna argue with you no more
> I've done it for too long.
>
> It was getting so good why then, where did it go?
> I can't think about it no more tell me if you know.
> You were loving me, I was loving you
> But now there ain't nothing but regretting
> nothing, nothing but regretting everything we do.
>
> I put up with your lies like you put up with mine,
> But God knows we should have stopped somewhere,
> we could have taken the time,
> But time has turned, yes, some call it the end.
>
> So tell me, tell me did you really love me like a friend?
> You know you don't have to pretend,
> It's all over now. It'll never happen again, no no no,
> it'll never happen again, it won't happen again
> Never, never, never, it'll never happen again
>
> No, no, no, no. . . .
> So maybe you're right, and maybe you're wrong
> But I ain't gonna argue with you no more
> I've done it for too long . . . ..
> You were loving me, I was loving you
> But now there ain't nothing but regretting everything we do.[13]

---

[12] "The Syzygy: Anima and Animus," *Aion*, CW 9ii, par. 30. (CW refers throughout to *The Collected Works of C.G. Jung*)

[13] "Maybe You're Right," on *Mona Bone Jackon* (2000); Ascap.

Well, however you look at it, breaking up is hard to do. As a matter of fact, I reckon I could write just as plausible an account of our relationship from B's perspective. But I will not go there, pleading conflict of interest—not to mention my complexes/blind spots. However, it is worth quoting the admonishment by noted Romantics scholar Ross Woodman, Professor Emeritus of English at the University of Western Ontario: "Don't let your fate become your destiny."[14] I take this to mean that fate is a chance turn of events, a random happening, inherently temporary, while destiny is the who-you-were-meant-to-be finale.

*

As a possibly irrelevant aside, I have recently been alerted to the devastating concept of "Death Ground" as espoused by the Chinese military strategist Sun Tzu in *The Art of War*. This tome was written in the sixth century BC, but apparently it has informed many modern combat operations and war-leaders of every stripe, and also contemporary businessmen. Here follows a taste of what I have learned, which may also be applicable to some relationship conflicts.

Military theorists define the point of no return in war as the "Death Ground," the place from which the only way out is to kill the enemy: ships burned, backs against the wall, retreat not possible; victory or death. After soldiers realize that, the ruthlessness of combat moves to a new level, and fighting to the death becomes natural. See it acted out in many World War Two movies and more recently in the film *300,* where a doomed contingent of brave Spartan soldiers stand their ground against some 10,000 Phoenecians.

The Death Ground is the most fearsome place in the world, yet, of course, it is not a place at all, but a state of mind. Where a military initiative may have first been organized to assure the well-being of one's group, on the Death Ground the very meaning of such well-being shifts, and now even survival can seem a lesser value. Honor or revenge or the feeling of mastery over one's destiny can matter more than life. Death

---

[14] Personal communication.

Ground makes no sense at all; it is senselessness itself, the very epitome of nonsense.

Nevertheless, Death Ground is a predictable pattern of war-making, a movement from the illusion that brutal force can be humane to the revelation that brutal force dehumanizes the victor and the vanquished alike. At a certain point in the escalation of violence, what began as a rational process, with clearly defined limits and purposes, becomes something else entirely.

In a definition offered by the historian Sue Mansfield, war "'refers to organized, premeditated, socially approved action involving groups of men in relatively complex operations of aggression and defense, and pursued in a rational fashion in order to accomplish certain goals."[15]

But the dynamic of war is such that inevitably, at the boundary of the Death Ground, the order implicit in such an idea completely breaks down. Organized activity becomes chaotic. Premeditation gives way to emotional reflex. Rage replaces strategy. Social approval falls before fear and shame. The goals for which war was begun are forgotten. War becomes its own goal. No-sense rules the roost.

In the Death Ground, warring parties who despise each other come to resemble each other, if not in tactics, in attitudes. Together they create the Death Ground by taking up positions from which, for psychological reasons as much as military ones, they cannot find ways of escape. Perception is the only reality, and each party becomes an aggressor in the firm belief that it is reacting to the aggression of the other.

Once the Death Ground is entered, the justice and virtue in the name of which each party began yield to the irresistible dynamic of war itself, which, despite martial (or marital) rhetoric, knows nothing of justice, nothing of virtue. In the immortal words of Matthew Arnold's "Dover Beach":

> And we are here as on a darkling plain,
> Swept with confused alarms of struggle and flight
> Where ignorant armies clash by night.[16]

---

[15] *The Gestalts of War,* p. 136.

[16] *The Norton Anthology of Poetry,* 3rd ed., p. 794.

I will not presume to know how the Death Ground might apply to your life and your relationships, but leave you to ponder on it, as I do.

****

Five
Harder They Fall

You may be wondering by now what the preceding pages have to do with Jungian psychology. Well, me too. Maybe I've lost my marbles, which I did often enough knuckling down on the playground in grade school. Nor was I much better at sports later, except when I led my high school volleyball team to a provincial championship in Halifax, Nova Scotia. But forget that; it just slipped out, I'm not stuck in the past.

The fact is, I have expostulated so often in my other books on the fundamental concepts of analytical psychology—persona, shadow, ego, animus/anima, Self, projection, etc.—that I tend to assume that the readers of this one are sufficiently sophisticated psychologically to read between the lines of the vignettes I present. This may be just wishful thinking, but it is tiresome to keep plagiarizing myself.

*

I am writing this book, or maybe just typing, but behind it all is the unseen hand of a guiding center in my psyche, playing me like a puppet. I am not master in my own house. I am a renter at best, my ego sharing space with a panoply of saints and knaves, nobles and villains, with a landlord more or less indifferent to the lot. I mean to say, we are answerable to a higher power whether we like it or not. You might call it God, Gnu, what have you. I call it the Self because it's part and parcel of my mental infrastructure as a Jungian analyst.

Meanwhile, I have recently discovered emolients, especially those frothy cleansers designed to moisturize your skin and prevent you from looking like a prune. (Well, they must work because I don't look like a prune; a peach, if anything.) I reckon they are the best invention since orange sticks for cleaning fingernails. Of course women have known all this since childhood. But few men are interested. I wonder, do they really want to look as ravaged as Clint Eastwood in *Gran Torino?*

Now, how did I get to an advanced age without knowing anything about emolients? I put it down to a misspent youth in the land of Logos, where the body is something you simply put up with or use, not nurture. Emolient-makers are handmaidens to the world of romance fostered by cosmetics, which is to say Eros, and every bit as seductively responsible for our Western culture as Tony Bennet, Frank Sinatra or Elvis Presley. I can say too that I am more sympathetic to the world of fashion after watching Shirley MacLaine's star turn in *Coco Chanel.*

Might I also tell you about *squalane?* Well, wild horses couldn't stop me. Never heard of it? Well, it's closer than you think. Apparently it is both a secretion that builds up daily alongside the nose and (crazy believe it) a component derived from shark's liver. That's just for beginners. When it is wiped away (from the nose) it becomes *squalene.* I read about this little-known fact in a detective thriller which I now forget the name of. But I thought I'd pass it on for readers who are fed up with psychology, as I am often enough to take pleasure in policiers. Well, whatever fuels your fire. As a teenager I read almost nothing but science-fiction, including *Amazing Comics* and *Captain Marvel.* My heroes were Isaac Asimov, Arthur C. Clark, Theodore Sturgeon and the publisher Hugo Gernsback, patriarch of the genre in the 1940s and 50s. I even created my own fanzine, an ambitious act of vanity if not exactly foolish nonsense. But it propelled me into life beyond Latin classes and parallel bars in the high school gym; for better or worse, who is to say. At my age I'm grateful to be able to read.

Okay, get a load of this mind-bender:

Squalene is a natural organic compound originally obtained for commercial purposes primarily from shark liver oil, though botanic sources are used as well, including amaranth seed, rice bran, wheat germ, and olives. All higher organisms produce squalene, including humans. . . It is a hydrocarbon and a triterpene.

In vaccine development, squalene has been used as an adjuvant, which increases the immune response of vaccines that would otherwise be too weak to offer protection. A squalene adjuvant was used in a cytomega lovirus vaccine. Some animal studies have found adverse effects, such as weakness, from squalene, and some veterans have claimed that squalene adjuvant in vaccines was responsible for Gulf War Syndrome.

Squalane is a saturated form of squalene in which the double bonds have been eliminated by hydrogenation. Because it is less susceptible to oxidation, it is more commonly used in personal care products than squalene.[17]

Indeed, what will they think of next?

While we're here, if you're still with me, I might as well tell you what I know or have read about ozone. It is possibly nonsense, but you can judge for yourself by Googling or Binging the word.

It is well known that ozone is an atmospheric layer that surrounds the earth and protects us from the full blast of the sun's rays, a layer we worry about destroying through the process of global warming. You may even have heard of ozone therapy, which touts the benefits of ingesting or injecting large amounts of it, but did you know that you can make it in your own bathroom?

Now, this is so top secret that it isn't even on Wikipedia, which carries so much other nonsense that you want to throw up.

Here is how it works. When you have a shower, the water out of the nozzle, H_2O, loses its H molecule to the air and, thanks to the miracle that is chemistry, acquires another two oxygen molecules, becoming O_3, which is the chemical composition of ozone. O_3 laves the open pores, and that, it is said, is why showers are refreshing as well as cleansing.

Now, I really know didley squat about *why* O_3 is more refreshing than H_2O, but it sounds like a process of transformation, and that's my business. Maybe someone will one day write a book on the psychology of ozone. Goofier things have happened.

Jeez, I feel like a caveman in face of the present, not to mention the unforeseeable future, which is bound to be scarier than anything Robert

---

[17] See Wikipedia. You can look up "adjuvant," "cytomega," and "triterpene" yourself.

Heinlein or Ray Bradbury envisaged. A recent pamphlet touting the wares of a phone company trumpets, "Meet the future. It's friendly." Well, I think that's just self-serving codswallop. They'll hit us with some handsome new gadget that we just *must have,* and it won't be any friendlier than a turnip. Betcher bottom dollar.

*

On my vial of sleeping pills, in red alert: **May cause drowsiness.** Holy petunia, what clever copywriter thought of that? Maybe the same smart-ass who penned the health-scare warnings on cigarette packs. We drown in declarations of the obvious.

Modern life is mystifying to me, and not because I'd like to have lived in another era. I am glad to be living in the present, but just think of it: no one ever asked if we wanted cell phones, email, MP3 players podcasts or virtual environments, Twitter, Facebook, Second Life, YouTube, Skype, blogs and so on. One day they were simply there. Why?

It's just because they could, says my digitally-savvy daughter JK, who earned a master's degree in computer science from the Naval Postgraduate School in Monterey while working for NASA on an other-worldly communications network via which earth-bound mortals could speak to, or email, astronauts in space; not to mention her involvement with the top-secret, enigmatic Cloud Project, which apparently has nothing to do with those fluffy cumuli in the sky.[18]

Speaking of Second Life and other such websites that purportedly promote "social networking," they do not currently permit overt sexual activity between avatars (shadowy personae), but you can bet it will come. Passive (watch or read) sexual activity is ubiquitous on the Internet, so interactive sex on the world wide web is simply the inevitable next step; always with parental controls, of course, for that is the American way.

---

[18] You can track JK on Twitter @jessykate, as I do, though the generation gap prevents me from understanding what she's up to. You can also Google "Cloud Project," and see how far that gets you.

I don't know whether to clap my hands or go hide in a closet. Meanwhile, is wheat germ really healthy? Bran flakes? Milk thistle? They put a man on the moon, but they haven't figured out if cow's milk is really good for you, or how to get all the toothpaste out of a tube. What next? A computer chip in the skull, on a fingernail? Cholesterol is essential for good health? Obesity saves lives? Salt? Sugar? Don't get me started. I've stopped reading the newspaper; it's just too scary, what with a new war or natural disaster somewhere every day, or a medical discovery that upsets the traditional or current applecart. And that's all on top of SARS, swine flu, global warming, melting glaciers and Big Foot sightings. Current reality has far outpaced science-fiction. I am hiding out, like any sensible ostrich.

Now, having got that rant off my chest, I must concede that I could hardly do without iTunes on my Mac. It is possibly the best invention since the toothbrush or orange sticks. iTunes is both an enhancement to my life and a nuisance. The opposites again. I love it that I can buy or listen to virtually anything that catches my fancy, but Holy Moley, it does keep me up late at night! If I'm not up Cripple Creek with The Band or feelin' groovy with Simon and Garfunkle, I'm in bed with Fleeetwood Mac and dreaming of romancing Stevie Nicks, or moondancing with Van Morrison. Or punching the air to a Sinatra tune or enthralled by Dave Brubeck. It is a struggle to leave the music and go to an empty bed. Well, I don't need to dwell on that, for who does not feel bereft without somebody to love? Of course, cats, dogs, turtles, gerbils and other animals can be lovable, but you know what I mean.

I know it is foolish nonsense, but that doesn't stop me. I also know that rolling my Drum cigs and drinking Scotch, listening to music and bouncing off the walls till halfway to dawn is not a healthy lifestyle, but on the other hand, I think, what if that's keeping me alive? The opposites again. Such issues are not something I was taught to address when I was training to become a Jungian analyst. So I am obliged to learn by living my own nonsense, if indeed that's what it is. I think a classic Jungian (which I purport to be) would dub my lifestyle an anima problem. And I agree, although my inner woman Rachel does not assail me in dreams (as she is historically wont to do when I'm going off-track).

Of course, I am free to choose. I can continue writing here and listening to Miles Davis and John Coltrane and Sinatra or Streisand, or go to bed. I am very fortunate to have little more stress or conflict in my life than that. When I think of how many have nothing to eat and nowhere to sleep, I am abashed. I volunteer to teach English and math to immigrants and offer free counseling to minorities; I give money to shelters for battered women and I adopt children in countries whose names I cannot spell, but it's never enough to assuage my middle-class feelings of guilt. I guess I could found AWB (Analysts Without Borders), but I am travel-averse and not at all group minded.

Okay, so I soldier on, trying to be oblivious to the many natural disasters and political turmoils all over the world. This in itself is a stressful undertaking, and as I've already said, why I shy away from reading newspapers. I do listen to the radio, and the current disaster in Haiti touches my heart (January, 2010), but I haven't seen much on television that I can watch with equanimity, other than documentaries on space travel, animal life and Disney cartoons. Oh, exceptionally, TCM (Turner Classic Movies) on cable can engage me with an early Bette Davis, John Wayne, Barbara Stanwyck, Janet Leigh or James Cagney movie. All such things are substitute fare, of course, for a warm and willing body. Well, as they say in gay Paree and Quebec, *ça va sans dire* (that goes without saying).

Now, here's an old jazz standard, just for the fun of it—surely some of the most poignant lyrics ever written for a lost love:

> What's new?
> How is the world treating you?
> You haven't changed a bit
> Lovely as ever, I must admit
> What's new?
>
> How did that romance come through?
> We haven't met since then
> Gee, but it's nice to see you again
> What's new?

Probably I'm boring you
But seeing you is grand
And you were sweet to offer your hand
I understand. Adieu!

Pardon my asking what's new
Of course you couldn't know
I haven't changed, I still love you so.[19]

I deeply regret that I cannot embed music into these pages, but just imagine being able to hear the music as you read the lyrics! Well, they infuse fragrance into fashion magazines, don't they? So one day, some clever guy or gal will figure out how to make pages sing. Maybe even my son Dave or daughter JK. Betcher bottom dollar.

Of course, what the world needs now is Eros, not more heroic nonsense. Thank you, John Lennon:

As soon as you're born they make you feel small,
By giving you no time instead of it all,
Till the pain is so big you feel nothing at all,
A working class hero is something to be,
A working class hero is something to be.
They hurt you at home and they hit you at school,
They hate you if you're clever and they despise a fool,
Till you're so fucking crazy you can't follow their rules,
A working class hero is something to be,
A working class hero is something to be.

When they've tortured and scared you for twenty odd years,
Then they expect you to pick a career,
When you can't really function you're so full of fear.
A working class hero is something to be,
A working class hero is something to be.
Keep you doped with religion and sex and TV,

---

[19] "What's New?"—as sung by Frank Sinatra; lyrics by Burke and Haggart; Ascap. Many great singers and instrumentalists have recorded this, but Wes Montgomery does an especially haunting guitar rendition on his album *Smokin' at the Half Note* (Verve Music Group, 2005).

And you think you're so clever and classless and free,
But you're still fucking peasants as far as I can see,

A working class hero is something to be,
A working class hero is something to be.
There's room at the top they are telling you still,
But first you must learn how to smile as you kill,
If you want to be like the folks on the hill,
A working class hero is something to be.
A working class hero is something to be.
If you want to be a hero well just follow me,
If you want to be a hero well just follow me.[20]

****

Six
Up for Grabs

Personal analysis is not the be-all and end-all in relationships. It may not end conflicts, and it may even aggravate the acrimony between mates. You may become more aware of what an idjit you are, but still sink deeper into the mud. You see, analysis does not claim to cure all ills, only to help understand them. What one does with the understanding is up to the individual.

My clients' general hope, or presumption, is that they will rediscover themselves through my fish-eye lens on their material (dreams, etc.). This is a hope I share but in the event can seldom fulfill. An analyst is a guide, not a god or a wizard. People come to me with specific problems and conflicts. In the process of dealing with such issues, we inevitably become companions on the road to a fuller life. It is a two-way street, and analysis can be deemed successful when the analyst is also changed.

Trained and certified analysts don't have the upper hand on truth or

---

[20] "Working Class Hero," lyrics by John Lennon; Ascap.

wisdom; they are themselves often still holding on by their fingertips. This does not mean they are unfit to work psychologically with others; indeed, on the contrary, their own precarious but mindful condition fits them admirably for the profession, which involves being alert to what the unconscious has to say.

Listening to the unconscious is the touchstone of Jungian analysis, and virtually the only approach to psychic distress that distinguishes it from any other form of so-called talk therapy. Its other unique focus, of course, is on rediscovering who we were meant to be.

Jungians hold to the belief that the unconscious manifests through dreams and synchronistic events (aka meaningful coincidences, like when you're reading a book about elephants and you look up to see one waltzing down the street). Anyone can record his or her dreams, but then what to do with them? The ego and other complexes always interfere with interpreting the symbolic content of dream images. That's why it is helpful to have a professional to dialogue with. Even close friends are little help in this regard, for, without being aware of it, they inevitably bring their own complexes (masked as opinions) and projections into the picture, making it ever more foggy.

*

Another battle for the Stanley Cup? Hey, what a bore. The media seem to think that everybody in Canada is nuts about hockey, and that's the Canadian persona they fervently perpetuate. Well, leave me out, thanks anyway. It is a sport that is so irredeemably violent, the touchstone of "macho," that I can hardly watch it without becoming complexed.

Actually, I haven't watched a hockey game since I was lying on the floor making out with my teenage sweetheart in the twinkling light of the telly. And that was almost sixty years ago. Now, if I happened to have a paramour who liked watching hockey, I'd go along with her, why not? Or soccer, baseball, curling, lawn bowling, tennis, ping-pong, whatever. I am not a tenderfoot; I will engage in whatever will fuel a relationship, though to be honest I draw the line at playing golf, which has left me cold ever since I caddied for my father at age fourteen.

Men are not deliberately fickle. I think they are generally inclined to be faithful to their mate. However, they can be swayed by instinct into the arms of another. As it happens, women seem more able to resist that instinct to couple, though they may choose to go with it, according to circumstances. Of course, this is just my opinion, not a scientifically verifiable fact.

Personally, I am singularly, seriously, serially monogamous—bar an occasional flirtatious lapse when my moon shadow comes out to play. I am not good husband material, but in a relationship I am an enthusiastic and faithful companion for as long as it lasts. Of course I can be distracted by a pretty woman, but what man cannot? That is instinctive and momentary. My heart always belongs to my current lover. I could sing it like Young Sassy (SarahVaughan):

> As you desire me, so shall I come to you,
> Howe'er you want me, so shall I be,
> Be it forever, or be it just a day,
> As you desire me, come what may.
> I doubt not but you will do what you will with me,
> I give my life to you 'cause you're my destiny.
> And now, come take me, my soul is yours.
> As you desire me, I come to you.
> And now, come take me, my very soul is yours,
> As you desire me, I come to you.[21]

Actually, between you and me, my problem is that I am a dyed-in-the-wool romantic, so when a woman gets under my skin I find it hard to get her out when we part. This leads to a lot of painful introspection, which is good in the long run, but meanwhile I'm broken and sad. It's the "meanwhile" that drives me up the wall—longing for a warm body, someone to love. They are apparently available aplenty on internet dating sites, but I am too introverted to get out there and explore the possibilities. More, I have been burned often enough that I don't fancy wading through another firestorm of a woman's personal agenda and undifferen-

---

[21] "As You Desire Me," on *Young Sassy,* disk. 3; Ascap.

tiated complexes. It does limit my options.

I was aggressively proactive as an extraverted young man, cocky and confident, but these days I am cautious and self-protective. I have sore feet, bad circulation, hair in my ears and a dodgy ticker. I take blood thinners so I bruise easily. I take enough vitamin D3 to fell a horse. I used to love to travel, but now I can hardly bear to leave home except for groceries. I don't exercise and don't eat enough vegetables. I'm told this is not a healthy life style, but on the other hand, as I've said already, it may be what keeps me alive. The opposites are always there. What I want or believe today may be anathema tomorrow. I read recently that eating more carbohydrates is the way to lose weight. And now there is talk of broccoli as a miracle food against cancer, and mammograms aren't worth the time of day. What will tomorrow bring—smoking is good for the heart!? Walking bad for the feet? Fiber bad for the soul?

There is no end to the nonsense we are fed by experts and the media. My illiterate peasant grandma Weist put her faith in Vaseline—a dollop a day kept the doctor away. She lived to ninety-four, playing bingo and euchre and smoking like a stevedore. I played stud poker with her and her cronies when she was ninety in an old-folks' home, and she cleaned me out with a flush against my three aces; I pretended I didn't see her palm a fifth spade from her sleeve.

Aging is not a pleasant experience. As Bette Davis famously said, "Getting old is not for sissies." Your mind and body start falling apart. You stumble and fall, forget your meds and want to sleep a lot. The routine work you used to enjoy becomes onerous. You often need a sedative to sleep, and seldom recall your dreams. You see cute buns on the street and know you aren't in that league (thinking: whoever invented skinny jeans deserves a noble prize). You like living alone, but often feel lonely. You don't want a live-in mate, but you'd like to have a loving companion to play Scrabble or chess with, or cuddle, whatever.

However, there are advantages to being a senior citizen. You can declare your views—where your energy wants to go—and friends and relatives accept that—though they may not see it as I do in a Jungian perspective. They might think I'm an idjit, but no one scolds me for my bad habits or reclusive, travel-averse lifestyle, or tries to cajole me into doing what I'd rather not. And my children are especially gracious in accepting me as I have become. Okay, they may note that I smoke or drink too much, but they don't push it.

This is a degree of freedom and respect I did not experience as a young man. Then I was inclined, if not explicitly obliged, to fall in with the plans of others in order to fit into collective expectations. Well, that was the corporate culture personified at P & G, long gone now in fact but not in memory. Did I mention that the office I used to work in is just down the street from where I now live? For a couple of years I lived the promiscuous and tortured life dramatized in the current hit TV series *Mad Men*. If I hadn't left I'd be either dead or CEO by now, or maybe both. As it is, I have a small analytic practice that gets me up in the morning and keeps me on my toes. I have the publishing business and I can find time to write nonsense halfway to dawn. I have no company pension so I live on my wits, one way or another. And if I should happen to have serious medical problems, the Canadian health care system will be there for me; betcher bottom dollar.

I think too of my grandsons, several cute-as-a-button three- and five-year-olds who scream and shout, run about and eat up all my Ritz Biscuits. They cacaphonize the swimming pool. I can understand and tolerate the commotion, but do I have to like it? Well, we haven't bonded. Little people are gremlins who disturb my essentially quiet, contemplative life. They sometimes call me Grumpa, for good reason. I can only look forward to the day when I can talk to them, and vice versa. Today Devon actually thanked me for giving him a cookie; that's a first. And Julian asked me why there was so much wood in my house (built circa 1900). I was speechless, because that's why I bought it and paid thousands to have the paint removed. Little boys have a lens on the world that is so far from what I can apprehend that they are effectively aliens, if not yet old enough to be bona fide terrorists. Now, little girls are something else (one granddaughter), trumped only by big girls.

Okay, enough of that. Here's some sentimental nonsense you may recall by the blind black magician Ray Charles:

41

Now, baby when you sigh
(when you sigh)
I wanna sigh with you
When you cry
(when you cry)
I wanna cry some, too.
Now, ain't that love
(ain't that love)
Oh, ain't that love that I feel
(that I feel)
In my heart for you.

When your friends
(when your friends)
Turn their back on you
I'll be here
(I'll be here)
Just to see you through.

Now, ain't that love
(ain't that love)
Ain't that love
Ain't that love, ooohhh now
Ain't that love
That I feel in my heart for you.

Now when you walk
(when you walk)
I wanna walk with you
When you talk
(when you talk)
Wanna talk some, too.
Now, ain't that love
(ain't that love)
Oh, ain't that love that I feel
(that I feel)
In my heart for you.

If you ever
(if you ever)

Ever need a friend
I'll be with you
(be with you)
Yes, until the end.
. . . .

Baby, won't you let me hold your hand
I want to squeeze you as tight as I can
Baby, don't you need me by your side
To protect you and be your guide
Baby, I'm so in love with you
I'd do anything you tell me to.

Now, ain't that love
Ain't that love
C'mon now, ain't that love, now
(oh, oh, oh, oh)
Ain't that love, baby that I feel
In my heart for you
Oh, that I feel in my heart for you.
Oh, that I feel in my heart for you.
Oh. . .[22]

****

Seven
No Time Blues

Now, I am admittedly beholden to computers in my daily personal and professional life, but the sometimes whimsical behavior of supposedly rational software programs can make me dizzy with frustration. Nor is

---

[22] "Ain't That Love"; Ascap.

the hardware reliable, given our culture of "built-in obsolescence" that keeps the economy rolling along. I have a still-working toaster my parents bought in 1950—built to take Wonderbread but not bagels—but nowadays few things mechanical last for even a generation. I recently replaced my dishwasher, and tiptoe around my stove, clothes washer and dryer (15 years).

Case in point:

Last night, or better said early this morning, halfway to dawn, my iMac, only three years old, refused to reboot. My mainstay helpmate, computer-whiz son Dave (SharpConnections.com) did his best to no avail. It is now in computer hospital and possibly headed for Nigeria or wherever defunct electronics end up these days. I finally went to bed in mourning.

My experience is not unique, rather the rule, since we humans came to depend on selenium chips smaller than a postage stamp to do all kinds of things heretofore unimaginable. The world beyond my fingertips is a mystery to me, and not of overwhelming interest, but I do suffer when it's inaccessible.

Of course I know this is a ridiculous reaction to my computer going down, but still, it constellates a complex and underscores the shameful excesses of the developed Western world. How selfish and pampered we are, while millions have no food, no water, no medicine, no shelter even.

What did cavemen do when they dropped their chisel or stone tablet down a crevasse? How did they communicate without their tools? Perhaps they went back to shouting at each other, as small children do.

Well, we too still have voice and can revert to the telephone, not to mention letter-mail, an almost forgotten art that deserves resurrection— but all that is so twentieth century, and so slow. And call-answer is so inhuman that it is hardly worth reverting to.

So where does that leave me/us? In the frigging wilderness, that's where. Up Cripple Creek without a paddle. I can't continue typing my manuscript, can't search Google, can't access my stock portfolio, can't read eBooks, can't listen to iTunes or watch YouTube, can't access email. It is worse than losing a pet dog or cat; more like losing a limb.

Talk about a computer complex! I tell myself that this is certainly a temporary setback, like when the power grid is overloaded and the lights go off. The experts fix things and the lights come on again, a modern miracle, however you look at it. Meanwhile, I will watch old movies on TV, clean the house, do the laundry, use pen and paper, and transcribe these scribblngs when my computer is eventually fixed or replaced, as my son will certainly make happen, whatever it takes.

God save America—from itself.

*

Two days later and the lights are back on—the computer doctors installed a new hard disk and restored all my backed-up data. I am in business and happy again, listening to Chet Baker and Bill Evans. The hospital even returned the dead hard disk so I can give it a decent burial. Cremation is apparently not an option. Of course, I had signed on as an organ donor, like Will Smith did in that fabulous film *Seven Pounds,* but I was told that iMacs don't have the right DNA, or bad karma, something like that.

****

Eight
Turning Turtle

It wasn't until I came across Jungian psychology that I got a handle on my inner workings and what from time to time troubled me—certain moods and behavior that upset me or others.

You need an eagle eye to spot your nonsense. It doesn't jump out at you. It is just there. It happens without you knowing what's going on. That guy or dolly who caught your eye at a coffee break—you might find yourself in bed with her (or him) and wonder how you got there. Or when the IRS calls to question a dinner you expensed, you shake your head in disbelief.

"Damn!" you say, "This is nonsense!"

And so it is, but to what end? That is the point. You think you're happily married, so what are you doing with a strange but willing lass giving you head? Men go off the rails when this happens. Women too, but I won't go there.

It is worth recalling here the hierarchic structure of the psyche according to the tenets of analytical psychology developed experientially by Jung after he became fed up with Freud's dogma and dived into his own depths.[23] The results are now available for all to read and ponder in his remarkable, beautifully-illustrated private journals, *The Red Book*.[24]

The *persona* is the honest and honorable aspect of ourselves, our best foot forward that we show to the outside world. The *ego* is the master of consciousness. The *shadow* is the flip side of the persona—that side of ourself we are ashamed of or embarrassed about, or don't know at all. The *anima* (in a man) and *animus* (in a woman) are contrasexual components of the psyche. All these are complexes, conglomerations of associations, subject to the aegis of the Self, the center and circumference of the psyche, which comprises both consciousness and the unconscious. Complexes are indeed the energy centers of the psyche, and the building blocks of the personality; without them we would not be human. Whether our complexes are positive or negative factors in our life depends more on our attitude toward them than their content.

I will not say much here about Jung's model of typology, except to note that I have studied and written about it at enough length to realize that I am still a novice and that the widely-used MBTI (Myers-Briggs Type Indicator) is a crock.[25]

Jung's typological compass is intellectually and emotionally satisfy-

---

[23] See "Confrontation with the Unconscious," in his *Memories, Dreams, Reflections*, pp. 170ff.

[24] Personally, as noted earlier, I am of two minds about this publication. On the one hand, it gives scholars, both pro and con Jung, much food for thought. On the other hand, it seems to me very invasive of Jung's private space. But the very fact that he didn't destroy these early journals suggests that he expected them to be published one day, if only to vindicate his lonely discoveries.

[25] See my *Personality Types: Jung's Model of Typology*.

ing, but so nuanced as to be difficult to use except subjectively. However, I can say with confidence that the great divide is between introversion and extraversion.

For instance, on the most basic level, you don't just "drop in" on an introvert. Without notice you risk a bemused or even cold reception. Extraverts, on the other hand, are more or less always ready with open arms for visitors. Extraverts are usually jolly, hail-fellows-well-met—me in early life, my brother still. Introverts hang back behind a bushel; they tend to live their nonsense in private rather than subject themselves to that of others. As well, introverts are not naturally adventurous, though they may stretch to be so in order to please a loved one.

Introverts enjoy their own company; they excel as librarians, historians, teachers, geologists, accountants, counselors, artists of all genres. Extraverts tend to eschew solitude; they enjoy the limelight and pursue extraordinary activities, animal, vegetable or mineral—find them among dilletantes, spelunkers, mountain climbers, sky-divers, oceanographers, bush pilots, etc., also motivational speakers, salespeople and entertainers of all stripes, as well as many musicians.[26]

Of course there are crossovers, and nothing can be said for sure. The natural disposition of each type is invariably obfuscated or distorted by personal complexes, hence a so-called inversion of type is not uncommon—where the introvert is a happy-go-lucky partygoer and the extravert a stay-at-home bibliophile. Well, we all have a shadow that is by definition contratypical, though it may surface only later in life. I can attest to that myself, having moved over the years from being a party animal to a stay-at-home denizen of the deep, as reclusive as J. D. Salinger. I began my foray into life as a staid thinking-sensation type, but now my mind is so active with possibilities (intuition) that I can hardly sleep without a pill/potion four nights out of seven. Now, this is a turnaround that I am just getting used to living with.

*

---

[26] My experience is that introverts may be more self-reflective, simply because they make time for it, but they don't have a monopoly on introspection.

There is much psychology spouted in the media these days, but even the "experts" seem not to have any knowledge of Jung's epochal understanding of what makes us tick. And politicians? Well, some few may seek analysis, but as a group—no way; power pursuits are more pressing than self-understanding.

I am familiar with the works of some self-professed gurus, spiritual counselors such as Deepak Chopra and Eckhart Tolle. I admire them and their zeal for raising consciousness. However, they disappoint in their superficiality: namely, their apparent indifference to, or ignorance of, the influence of the unconscious, which to my mind must be included in any consideration of enlightenment. They are particularly prone to ignoring the shadow, which plays such a prominent role in our day-to-day life.

The work of C. G. Jung has the psychological depth that "spiritual enlightenment" gives lip service to but lacks in its pursuit of wholeness. I do not even care for the term "spiritual enlightenment," preferring the more modest goal of "psychological awareness."

So I ask you, without Jung's vision of the structure of the psyche—conscious and unconscious, shadow, persona, animus/anima—where are we? I am afraid that we are left with either opinions based on inexact science or rats behaving in mazes as they are expected to. Thus academic psychology has little to do these days with "psyche" (Greek for soul), and more's the pity.

Freud's views and psychoanalytic techniques have by now been more or less discredited. I believe it is high time that Jung's ideas were taken seriously by the mainstream and adapted for teaching in schools and universities. I think it is shameful that Jung is hardly mentioned in academic departments of psychology. He is generally dismissed as a whacko or a mystic, and taught, if at all, in departments of religion.

This is not right, but it will take educators who have personally experienced the precepts of Jungian psychology to change the picture.

****

Nine
Con Te Partiro

I am of an age when I can get away with considerable nonsense without being arrested.

My favorite teller at my TD bank is a petite lass with freckles and curly black hair down to her shoulders. She personifies cute and has a beguiling smile no matter the weather or time of day. I think of her as Dickens' Little Dorrit. Her name is actually something like Melinda or Sasha; I always forget. She recently emigrated from New Delhi. She has a red dot on her brown forehead, which I suppose marks her as one of a particular caste.

I shamble up to the wicket and plop down my weekly deposit book.

"Ms. Dorrit," I say, tipping my beret, " good to see you."

"Ayesha," she says, pointing to her name-tag. "I'm well, thanks, and yourself?"

"Never felt better," I lie. "You are so pretty. Are you free for lunch? And can you stay the night?"

Ayesha stops leafing through my deposit checks and leans forward. "Dr. Razr, you are a valued customer, but I am not otherwise available to you. I am a married woman!"—tapping her ring finger like it was the Grail.

"Oh, pardon me," I back off. "You see, you are numinous to me, but it is not your fault. I see you as a nymph out of place in this granite cell-block. Things go on in my head that I can't always control... I am not crazy, just complexed."

Dorrit/Ayesha rolls her eyes and seems about to call Security. But then she smiles, handing me back my deposit book. "Dr. Razr, you speak in tongues, will there be anything else?"

"Much more," I whisper as I slink away. Stephen Leacock couldn't do it better.[27]

---

[27] See "Banking," in Leacock, *Sunshine Sketches of a Little Town.*

Ten
Only the Lonely

This section is especially for those who have not had the pleasure of reading my *Jung Uncorked,* especially Books Two and Four, in which a character named Ms. Cotton Pants makes brief but significant appearances. My recountings are a touch audacious, a notch above what you'd find in a Harlequin romance, albeit provocatively erotic and not for the feint of heart. I used her in context to make specific psychological points, but she still qualifies as a manifestation of my nonsense. How foolish is for others to say.

I must prepare the ground with Jung's dissertation on the alchemical spirit Mercurius. To wit:

> In my contribution to [this symposium] I will try to show that this many-hued and wily god did not by any means die with the decline of the classical era, but on the contrary has gone on living in strange guises through the centuries, even into recent times, and has kept the mind of man busy with his deceptive arts and healing gifts.[28]

> One simple and unmistakable term in no way sufficed to designate what the alchemists had in mind when they spoke of Mercurius. It was certainly quicksilver, but a very special quicksilver, "our" Mercurius, the essence, moisture, or principle behind or within the quicksilver—that indefinable, fascinating, irritating, and elusive thing which attracts an unconscious projection.[29]

Mercurius, as the above passages imply, is one of the most elusive figures or concepts in the whole alchemical canon, for he is at once a chemical substance, a trickster and a spiritual essence that pervades all aspects of the alchemists' *opus.*

Jung begins his discussion with a detailed analysis of the Grimm fairy

---

[28] "The Spirit Mercurius," *Alchemical Studies,* CW 13, par. 239.
[29] Ibid., par. 259.

tale, "The Spirit in the Bottle," a medieval story so widely known in other versions and traditions that it qualifies as an archetypal motif. The essentials are briefly stated as follows:

> A poor woodcutter's son roaming the forest comes upon a massive old oak. He hears a voice calling from the ground: "Let me out, let me out!" The boy digs down and discovers a sealed glass bottle from which apparently the voice has come. He opens it and instantly a spirit rushes out and soon becomes as big as the oak. Now this spirit howls that he will have his revenge for being confined in the bottle, and he threatens to strangle the lad. The boy, being quick witted, conceives of a trick. "First," he says, "you must prove to me that you are the same spirit that was shut up in that little bottle." The spirit agrees and shrinks meekly back into the flask. The boy immediately seals it and the spirit is caught again.
>
> Now the spirit promises to reward the boy richly if he will let him out. The lad does so and is rewarded with a small piece of rag. The spirit says, "If you spread one end of this over a wound it will heal, and if you rub steel or iron with the other end it will turn into silver." The boy rubs his damaged axe with the rag and the axe turns to silver which he subsequently sells for a small fortune that enables him to go on with his studies. The rag works on wounds too and the boy later becomes a rich and famous doctor.[30]

Jung treats this tale as he would a dream or a fantasy—as a spontaneous statement of the unconscious about itself. He thereupon proposes a rather ingenious interpretation of its various elements, an elucidation which may strike some readers as whimsical, while those familiar with the intuitive, right-brain method of amplification will surely applaud:

> The fairytale mentions the forest as the place of the magic happening. The forest, dark and impenetrable to the eye, like deep water and the sea, is the container of the unknown and the mysterious. It is an appropriate synonym for the unconscious. . . . Trees, like fishes in the water, represent the living contents of the unconscious. Among these contents one of special significance is characterized as an "oak." Trees have individuality. A tree, there-

---

[30] Ibid., condensed; paraphrased from Grimm Brothers, *The Complete Grimm's Fairy Tales,* pp. 458ff.

fore, is often a symbol of personality. . . . The mighty old oak is proverbially the king of the forest. Hence it represents a central figure among the contents of the unconscious, possessing personality in the most marked degree. It is the prototype of the *self,* a symbol of the source and goal of the individuation process. The oak stand for the still unconscious core of the personality, the plant symbolism indicating a state of deep unconsciousness. . . . From this it may be concluded that the hero of the fairytale is profoundly unconscious of himself . . . . not yet "enlightened." For our hero, therefore, the tree conceals a great secret.

The secret is hidden not in the top but in the roots of the tree, and since it is, or has, a personality it also possesses the most striking marks of personality—voice, speech, and conscious purpose, and it demands to be set free by the hero. . . . The roots extend into the inorganic realm, into the mineral kingdom. In psychological terms, this would mean that the self has its roots in the body, indeed in the body's chemical elements. . . . The alchemists described their four elements as *radices,* corresponding to the Empedoclean *rhizomata,* and in them they saw the constituents of the most significant and central symbol of alchemy, the *lapis philsophorum,* which represents the goal of the individuation process.[31]

Wait, there's more:

The secret hidden in the roots is a spirit sealed inside a bottle. Naturally it was not hidden away among the roots to start with, but was first confined in a bottle, which was then hidden. Presumably a magician, that is an alchemist, caught and imprisoned it. As we shall see later, this spirit is something like the numen of the tree, its *spiritus vegetativus,* which is one of the definitions of Mercurius. As the life principle of the tree, it could also be described as the *principium individuationis* [principle of individuation].[32]

Jung sums up the foregoing as follows:

So if we translate it into psychological language, the fairytale tells us that the mercurial essence, the *principium individuationis,* would have developed freely under natural conditions but was robbed of its freedom by de-

---

[31] Ibid., pars. 241f.

[32] Ibid., par. 243.

liberate intervention from outside, and was artfully confined and banished like an evil spirit.[33]

And if that was so, asks Jung, who deemed the spirit to be evil and confined and banished it? Why, the Catholic Church of course, and Christianity in general with its doctrine of original sin and contempt for the body as the root of all evil. Jung's thesis is therefore that the magician/alchemist, in cahoots with his *soror mystica* (female assistant), hid the genie/spirit to protect it from the inhospitable cultural environment and provide an earthy spirit compensatory to the Church's designation of Christ as Logos. Hard to swallow? Well, read on.

Merurius is the fly in the ointment, the invisible little guy who ruins your plans. He is mercurial, after all, quite unpredictable; there's no telling when he might pop up in your life to turn it topsy-turvy, from driving you into a lamp-post to having a go at the baby sitter. And you can be conscious of his trickster quality and still be at his mercy. Mercurius is second cousin to the aliens who abduct you from hot tubs and break your ankles.

Of course, like any archetypal entity Mercurius embodies the opposites, and so he has a benign side as well. He gets you out of bed in the morning; he gives you ambition, ideas "out of the blue," a job to do, a mate to love, kids to focus on with awe.

Now I give you George, successful advertising executive in his mid-forties, happily married with three grown sons. He came to see me because he was obsessed with a young woman he barely knew. In our third session together he showed me a letter he had written her:

Dear Ms. Cotton Pants,
It is close to midnight, an ungodly hour to exorcise demons, but I have to declare myself. I have torn myself away from Hitchcock movies on the television to tell you that I am besotted with you.
    You may not remember me. Well, that's no surprise. You wouldn't notice me in a crowd, and we only brushed shoulders once at a concert hall

---

[33] Ibid., par. 244.

some months ago. I saw the moon in your eyes and I was immediately smitten, don't ask me why. I tracked you down and I have stalked you ever since. Oh, don't be afraid, I mean you no harm.

Now, I don't wish to be importunate, but I must see you in order to stay sane. Perhaps we can meet some day for coffee and a bagel. Please say yes, it would mean so much to me. I can be reached at Butterfield 9062, any time of day or night. Just ask for George. Please help! I am desperately in love with you.

"I haven't sent it," said George, tearfully. "I wanted to talk to you first." He showed me a picture of a cute seventeen-year-old.

Of course I cannot divulge details of our subsequent conversations, but I can say that George was relieved to hear that his plight was not unique and that he was not certifiably crazy. He gladly absorbed what I told him about the phenomenon of projection, and he was open to the possibility of a feminine side of himself that he saw in "Ms. Cotton Pants," a fanciful moniker he associated with a teenage girlfriend, a cheerleader who brazenly flashed her undies in public but locked knees in private. He also confessed that when watching movies he often imagined her in the role of the heroine. In short, he took seriously the image of Ms. Cotton Pants as an inner woman he needed to get to know.

Well, it was not long before George stopped obsessing about Ms. Cotton Pants and turned his attention to his wife, who responded to his ardor as never before.

*

Well, as it happens, I had some dealings with this winsome lovely a few years after George stopped seeing me. She turned up one afternoon in the back row of a university lecture hall in which I was teaching a class in Alchemy 101. There was no mistaking Ms. Cotton Pants—still cute, identifiably a thirty-something excheerleader, underdressed in skimpy tank top and tight tartan mini-skirt. She could hardly sit still and seemed intensely interested in my discourse, occasionally voicing her appreciation. She smiled at me and waved when the class was over.

Now, there's no denying that such a woman was tailor-made to engage my attention at that time in my life. I was thirty-eight years old, half-bald, divorced, lonely, penniless and going nowhere in the academic world. I was crazy about Jung and had fantasies of going to Zurich to train as an analyst. However, I forgot about Ms. Cotton Pants until a few days later when she came to my office.

She knocked and sidled in wearing the same provocative outfit.

"Dr. Razr," she said, "am I disturbing you?"

"Not at all," I replied rather grumpily, for I was cozily engaged in self-pity. "Please, have a seat."

Ms. Cotton Pants considered the options and chose a straight-back wing-chair. She sat and unlocked her knees, revealing what might be called her alter ego, Ms. Cotton Pant-less.

My mood changed. My *puer* woke up. Mercurius stirred. Projections were flying. I was acutely in need of a *soror mystica* to save me from the madness of the lead—someone more physically accessible than the elusive, ethereal Rachel. I moved to the couch and patted a cushion. "You'll be more comfortable here," I smiled.

In a trice she was beside me with her head tucked under my chin. Her hands roved up and down my body. I fondled her elfin ears. "I just love psychology!" she cooed, "but what does it all mean, and is alchemy practical?"

I affected a worldly manner. "Well, I could tell you astonishing tales of the *tertium non datur,* the *sine qua non* and the medieval Axiom of Maria, but that would be getting ahead of ourselves, so first," I said, guiding one of her hands lower, "the *prima materia."*

Ms. Cotton Pants tentatively explored the bulging front of my trousers. "It's alive!" she cried.

"You betcher cotton panties," I agreed, "and he speaks!"

Then we heard a voice: "Let me out! Let me out!"

Ms. Cotton Pants beat me to the zipper, and out popped Mercurius, gnarled, in a sealed vessel as long as an arm.

"Holy petunia!" whooped Ms. Cotton Pants, "it's a retort!"

"Cooped up in the *vas* these many months," I observed.

"I have had my punishment and I will be avenged!" cried Mr. M.

The wily Ms. Cotton Pants considered. "Fair enough," she said, "but first prove that you big fella were actually in that small space."

Mr. M shriveled back in. Ms. Cotton Pants zipped me up and he was caught again. Now Mr. M promised to reward her richly if she let him out. "Release me and I will repay you with precious gems and the secret of the *filius philosophorum!*"

Ms. Cotton Pants unzipped me again and whipped her tight skirt off with a whistle. Mr. M. rushed out with gusto and nudged her pretty pudendum. "Let me in, let me in!" he cried.

Ms. Cotton Pants gasped as she angled herself to receive the twisted root. After a few minutes she got up, slipped her undergear back on and left without a word. Mr. M retreated to his lair.

I never saw Ms. Cotton Pants again that semester, in or out of class, but much later I read that in her guise as the esteemed Dr. Vivian Flatbush, director of the Burgholzli Clinic in Zurich, she was awarded the Nobel prize in medicine for discovering a cure for schizophrenia.

I sent her flowers, the least I could do.

*

[I did get into some trouble with Rachel for the foregoing; We were discussing the nature of creativity and she suggested it was a divine attribute; I demurred, viz:]

"Don't you see?" I said. "It's a complex that drives people to create. It's actually in the same category as collecting stamps or coins or matchbook covers."

Rachel found that hard to swallow. "So artists are neurotic, is that it? Art is the result of neurosis?"

I gnashed my teeth.

"Dearest, you misunderstand the nature of a complex. A complex is a feeling-toned idea that gets you by the throat. It's only neurotic when it gets in the way of your life. You can be stimulated to create because of a complex, but what you produce still has to be shaped. You can't do that unless you have some distance from the complex. Granted, there are creative people who would do better work if they weren't neurotic. And there are neurotics whose creativity is locked in the closet of unconsciousness. Complexes are the key. Understand your complexes and it's a whole new ball game."

Rachel mused about that. "Where do I fit in?"

"You're the bridge to what's going on in me. You mediate the contents of my unconscious. Without you I'd have nothing to work with. Thanks to you, it wells up in me. It's all there, I can see it. But it has to be given an appropriate form. That's my job, alternately exciting and disheartening, and always threatened by the madness of the lead. Ms. Cotton Pants is a case in point."

Rachel snapped: "Well, now that you mention it, I haven't recovered from your writings on that vixen. She wasn't my doing. I suppose you see her as a metaphor, but I was stunned by the sheer audacity of it. And what's the point of such prurience in a book that purports to be a serious appraisal of Jung's work?"

I shrugged. "I'm not sure, but perhaps to alert the reader to the shadowy reality behind the writer who is writing, a real person who is not just an automaton mouthing Jung. Once in a while, you know, I have an original thought."

"Still," said Rachel, "it is outrageous nonsense."

"I'll give you that," I replied. "Ms. Cotton Pants is a daring conceit, but my account is symbolically true to what I know of the male psyche, and true too to my own enigmatic process of individuation. I will not gainsay myself. I like what I've made of Ms. Cotton Pants, so she stays. That's hubris, don't I know it, but what the hell, I'm just a pawn, after all. And you are so beautiful."

Rachel sniffed. "Now you stop that!"

I busied myself twisting paper clips into stick men while Rachel calmed down. I felt a bit uneasy because I was not used to opposing Rachel; usually I give way to her, not just to keep the peace but because she generally knows better.

"Okay," she said finally, "I think I get it. Ms. Cotton Pants is a complex of yours and you chose to play with it. But what starts the creative process? What sparks the complex?"

I leaned back. I could speak of archetypes, the collective unconscious;

I could give examples from fairy tales, mythology and religion. I could cite literature from all over the world. Yes, like Jung I could babble on for a hundred pages and come back to square one.

"I don't know," I said. "It's a mystery to me."

Rachel smiled. "That's what I said in the first place—*God.*"

*

[Finally, in *Jung Uncorked,* Book Four, Ms. Cotton Pants came up again in a discussion of Jung's magnum opus, *Mysterium Coniunctionis,* as follows.]

I am sorely tempted here to resurrect Ms. Cotton Pants, the pneumatic young lady I plucked from obscurity earlier in this series. She has been much on my mind as I re-read this section of Jung's major work on alchemy. My interest is not prurient, but rather pragmatic, and so I will not resist her reappearance.

You may recall that I used her personable antics metaphorically, anecdotally, archetypally, in explicating the significance of Mercurius in the alchemical *opus* and the human psyche. It is true that some readers found it crude and tasteless, but others conceded it to be appropriate for the context, albeit somewhat risqué for a book of a purported serious nature.

One irate reader said I should be defrocked. A friend counterpunched: "Better to have loved and been defrocked than never to have frocked at all." Which put me in mind of Jung's admonition: "If you don't live your nonsense you will never have lived at all, and the meaning of life is surely that it is lived, not avoided."[34] Anyway, the Jungian community doesn't defrock analysts, just condemns them to reading their own books over and over and over.

Be that as it may, since Ms. Cotton Pants' induction into the Nobel hall of fame for her mature work on schizophrenia, we have spent many a pleasant soirée together playing backgammon or discussing the nature of the Pleroma, which for her is like playing chess with a toad.

Pragmatically, any *coniunctio* requires a vis-à-vis, a partner. More, a willing participant in the dance of the senses, or alternatively, as in my

---

[34] *Visions: Notes of the Seminar Given in 1930-1934,* p. 1147.

loverNot relationship with Cottie (as I have come to call her), an appreciation of the bizarre and absurd, as evidenced for instance in my book *Chicken Little: The Inside Story,* featuring Professor Adam Brillig, which Cottie found enchanting, intriguing, and an adventure worthy of Indiana Jones. I know this because her doctoral thesis, "The Barnyard as a Source of *Concupiscence*," quoted generously from my own forays into the fowl psyche. Indeed, I only dissuaded her from becoming a card-carrying Chickle-Schticker on the basis of her precarious academic situation, where misogynous colleagues are ever on the lookout for aberrant impulses on the part of female faculty.[35]

As noted above, Ms. Cotton Pants, in her ascension to the airy heights of academe, did not forsake her earthy background or supportive friends such as myself. Thus I trust she will not mind if I divulge one of her favorite tunes from the sixties, when she was deeply involved in the peace movement, free love and alternative lifestyles:

> Slow down, you're moving too fast,
> you got to make the morning last,
> just kicking down the cobblestones,
> looking for fun and feeling groovy.
> Ba da da da da da da, feeling groovy.
> Hello lamppost, whatcha knowing?
> I've come to watch your flowers growing.
> Ain't ya got no rhymes for me?
> *Doo doo doo doo,* feeling groovy.
> I got no deeds to do, no promises to keep.
> I'm dappled and drowsy and ready to sleep.
> Let the morning time drop all its petals on me,
> Life I love you, all is groovy.
> *Doo doo doo doo,* feeling groovy.[36]

To be fair, Cottie sometimes seems a little piqued when at the end of an intimately imaginative evening playing Scrabble, say, or listening to

---

[35] Chickle-Schtick is the area of academic research that focuses on fears of the end of the world, exemplified by Chicken Little's dire warning that the sky is falling.

[36] Simon and Garfunkle, "The 59th Street Bridge Song (Feeling Groovy)"; Ascap.

Beethoven or Charlie Parker, I debouche to my separate sleeping quarters; but she is not forward and does not force the issue. Truth to tell, I often wish she would, for a lone *coniunctio* is a sad oxymoron, a pale shadow of the real thing. I do desire her, and I am hopelessly in love with the image of her in my head, but I respect her attachment to her husband, the esteemed Professor Emmanuel Flatbush, head of the department of endocrinology at the University of Toronto, and anyway she is really much too smart for me.

I can add that I have learned a lot from Cottie; particularly that an erotic attraction need not be acted out, nor even sublimated (according to Freudian theory), but may transform into a transcendent relationship that surpasseth all understanding.

****

Eleven
Eat Your Heart Out

Well, what next? I have a notebook full of nonsense, and it's not easy to choose. What belongs here? What doesn't?

It is always a struggle for me to stop writing and go to bed. I have to become somewhat unconscious when I write, otherwise I am trapped in Logos. And if I'm rolling with Eros in the midst of the night, halfway to dawn, I like to keep going, for I never know what the morrow will bring—if I can recapture the mood and flow I abandoned for sleep. My practice, then, is not to exit the computer without leaving a snippet to pursue the next day—a few words, a line or two.

So, this morning I came back to find this:

"Win some, lose some."

Oh yes, that put me back on track. I had been watching *Let's Get Lost,* the Bruce Weber documentary about the life of the legendary jazz trumpeter Chet Baker. This film, and Chet Baker's playing, enthralls me. During the 1950s and 60s, together with other such greats as Gerry Mul-

60

ligan, Stan Getz, Dizzy Gillespie, Miles Davis and Charlie Parker, he furthered the movement out of bebop into what came to be known as "cool, west coast" jazz. He was as famous in his musical genre as the Beatles were in pop.

The young Chet Baker was a handsome, charismatic James Dean lookalike. His father, a professional guitarist, gave him a second-hand trumpet when Chet was eleven, and young Chet taught himself to play, says his mom in the film, by listening to music on the radio. Apparently he was a natural—seldom practiced, but put the horn to his lips and out flowed honey; he was the king bee trumpeter of his time, as revered as Miles Davis. Chet was an accomplished singer too—at once both husky and mellow—but always better known for his expertise with a horn. I never experienced him in person, but I treasure the memory of Miles Davis in Toronto in 1970 as he leaned back and disappeared into the music. He defined and personified the term "laid back."

Chet Baker had many admirers during his ascent to fame in his twenties. He played all over North America and Europe, but by the age of thirty he was doing coke and heroine heavy duty. His life thereafter was turbulent both emotionally and creatively. At fifty he was exhausted and physically ravaged by drug use, though no less charismatic. He went on to record some of his best works, then died at the age of fifty-eight, falling out of a hotel window in Amsterdam...

It seems to me such a sad life and waste of talent, but who am I? I wasn't there, he was. Wow, talk about living your nonsense. Chet Baker did it in spades, for which he paid a heavy price, as did some of those who loved him, including two ex-wives. The latter in this film are very gracious, praising him for who he was, no blame.

Did Chet Baker individuate? It is an interesting, troubling and open question, as it is for most of us. "I'm always looking for my life," he says at age fifty-seven in a candid moment on camera. What more can one ask? He was not overtly psychologically aware, but few artists are. They do their thing and the devil take the hindmost. They cut themselves out of the herd and live with the consequences—fame and fortune, or poverty and disdain, or something in between.

From my perspective, the trumpet was Chet Baker's anima, his soul. She was a bitch goddess—she took him into creative waters, then drowned him with drugs. This can happen to artists of any kind, not to mention accountants, teachers, athletes, plumbers and the like—well, few of us are immune to addiction of one kind or another, if only to escape, or keep up with, the hectic pace of modern life.

Personally, I am addicted most of all to reading—not just books but billboards, license plates, toothpaste tubes, store fronts, packaging of any kind. Canada being bilingual, half my vocabulary in French comes from reading the other side of cereal boxes. My mind may go to sleep, but my eyes never rest. This is nonsense, for sure, but what is one to do. You bin a leopard born with some spots. You gotta accept who you are, or pretend otherwise and become neurotic. I mean, I don't fall in love so easily, but I am a sucker for a warm and willing body.

Chet Baker sings it:

> Let's get lost, lost in each other's arms
> Let's get lost, let them send out alarms
> And though they'll think us rather rude
> Let's tell the world we're in that crazy mood.
>
> Let's defrost in a romantic mist
> Let's get crossed off everybody's list
> To celebrate this night we found each other, mmm, let's get lost
>   [horn solo] [piano solo]
>
> Let's defrost in a romantic mist
> Let's get crossed off everybody's list
> To celebrate this night we found each other, mm, let's get lost
> oh oh, let's get lost.[37]

****

---

[37] "Let's Get Lost"; Ascap.

Twelve
Eponymous Sludge

It is the month of June, 1963. I am twenty-seven years old. B and I are living with our two-year-old son in half an idyllic English country cottage in Devon. Friends come from London to visit. Our landlady next door is pleasant. I go off each day to contend with four-to-eight-year-olds in a local grade school. I am supposed to teach them the three R's and help civilize them. It is a task I fail miserably at, but meanwhile B gives birth to a strapping future squash player, whom I deliver just as our doctor arrives in his new white Saab. We name this new fella Ben.

I am desperate for a break. I see an ad in the *New Statesman* for a nanny wanted to go to a Greek island and look after the kids of Penelope Mortimer (author of *The Pumpkin Eater,* wife of John, author of the series *Rumpole of the Bailey.)* I apply. I hear back from Mrs. Mortimer two weeks later. She is sorry but I just don't sound right for a nanny, and it would be a shame for me to leave my young family for three months.

I am disappointed but I leave my young family anyway, though only for a month. I pack a sack with a change of clothes and my typewriter. B is not unhappy to be left with two little ones; she is a natural-born mother and glad to be rid of my importunate advances. I am a frisky, adventurous puer, horny as a moose. I set off to hitchhike around Europe, seeking a quiet youth hostel where I can edit and retype my latest magnum opus, *Notebooks of a Prodigal Son.* You understand, redrafting a manuscript was not simple in those days, way before personal computers. And before typewriters, it was worse; there was only stone on stone and then quill and quire. How many stones did it take to write a book? How many quills and quires?

Hitchhiking on the Continent was pretty safe in the 1960s. I got lucky and within a week I was ensconced in a modest castle somewhere in the heart of France, on the *Route du Grand Cru* (Road of Great Wines), near Dijon. A lovely lady, 40ish, drove me there and asked if she could stay the night. I have become travel-averse, but I have never been averse to such an invitation. However, she came to her senses in the middle of the night and drove away.

Before that, though, there was a twenty-year-old madchen in Germany who picked me up on her bicycle. She took me for a swim in a pond, and then home for the night to her bewildered parents. I was sorely tempted to take advantage of her apparent innocence, but I just couldn't do it, and we parted the next day with a smile.

And I mustn't forget Bruno, wealthy steel magnate who picked me up in Dusseldorf and took me into his home in Bad Kreuznach. I abused his hospitality by sexually assaulting his maid in the middle of the night. She told her employer and Bruno was so enraged I thought he might shoot me. Jeez, what nonsense I was prone to in those days, when my right hand didn't know what my left was doing.

Anyway, within two weeks I had finished my retype, rolled it up like toilet paper, and set off for home. The first ride I got was with a businessman on his way to Madrid. He was a maniacal driver, and I begged to get out before we hit the Tyranees. Then I made my way slowly up the west coast of France to the ferry back to Dover.

B welcomed me back, but not as the lover I longed to be. I was put into service changing diapers and making meals. No blame to B. Life is not a lot of fun with a crawler and a toddler demanding attention. Not to mention a needy, narcissistic, love-sick husband.

In September I resumed teaching young terrorists. In October our landlady evicted us, saying her son needed a place to live. We packed all our belongings into our old green Ford van and drove off to London, abandoning our yellow-eyed black cat Smokey along the way. I've always felt guilty about that.

We had no destination in mind—though we could have stayed with friends in a pinch—until en route I read another ad in the *New Statesman*. This one sought tenants for a seventeeth-century cottage in West Sussex; the rent was five pounds a week. We stopped at a pub and I phoned. The landlady, Prunella, was responsive to our plight and we sealed the deal.

We rolled into Heyshott, a hamlet of some two hundred souls about three hundred miles south of London. For a young North American couple, Laurel Cottage was a dream home. True, it was rather primitive and not too well insulated, but it was like living in Shakespeare's time. It was opposite the village green and right next door to the local pub. I liked the pub, but the publican, an ex-major in the Royal Air Force, treated me like a child and I could never stand up to him. Talk about a father complex.

But B got on well with his wife and soon found work there helping in the kitchen. Our two boys were bussed to school, and I had most days free to write in a small shed at the foot of the garden, connected to the house by a tinkle bell on the end of a clothesline. I picked up an M.A. in Modern European Studies at the University of Sussex in Brighton, and sometimes I worked as a postman; best job I ever had. It was all pretty romantic in theory, but in reality it was a tough slog because B always wanted me to be someone else.

*

We lived in Laurel Cottage for the next six years, with eight months away in Dijon, France, where I did a postgraduate degree researching the work of Jean-Jacques Rousseau while teaching English in the university there. Well, that's another story, with its men-only, six-hour, five-course dinners once a month soaked in great wines of the region.

We left Heyshott, with considerable regret, to live in B's inherited homestead in Burlington, Ontario. We intended to return soon to our quiet village life. But it didn't work out that way, as I have recounted here earlier. Back in Canada I was grabbed by the "cultural revolution" and B became ever more distant. Finally my fate was sealed when I got high with my secretary and took her to that Rolling Stones concert. Well, I don't need to dwell on that nonsense, except to say that it propelled me into a world where I again felt loved.

I don't look back in anger. I just do what is right in front of me. Betcher bottom dollar.

✸✸✸✸

Thirteen
Dolce Vita

My nonsense these days has more to do not with sexual issues but with health care.

As you age, monitoring the state of your eyes, ears, nose and throat, heart, liver, kidney and bowels is a full-time job. You can go mad racing to doctors' appointments, and if you're not late, they are. You get chest x-rays, colonoscopies, angiograms, blood tests for PSA, INR, iron and other minerals. You fret about getting enough vitamins and fiber, taking in too much salt or sugar, or not enough, and the possibility of diabetes. Sometimes you forget to take your meds. You have a dodgy ticker, clogged arteries and sore feet. You are ripe for a stroke or a heart attack. So you live one day at a time, always somewhat surprised when you wake up not dead.

You'd like to stop smoking and drinking, but you wonder if in fact they are keeping you alive, for they're the only relief you have from worrying about when you might collapse and not get up. Your mate (if you're lucky enough to still have one) is pretty much fed up with hearing about your ailments, and similarly you have given up tracking hers. You don't have the stamina to travel or walk any distance, and you don't remember how to play bridge. Your old friends are dead, demented or firmly embedded in the Pleroma. Your children are grown up and busy with their own lives. You introvertedly eschew support groups, so manage on your own as best you can. Once in a while you think of jumping offa bridge, but it passes.

Jeez, what a gawdawful scenario. Pardon me for painting such a depressing picture. Of course old age needn't look or feel like that. It is simply the darkest possibility, and I wanted to get it out of the way before I moved on to celebrate the wonders of still being alive after retiring.

Personally, I really have nothing to complain about—stable health, meaningful work, close friends and loving children. Of course, I would like to have a paramour, but I won't belabor that. Most lives lack something, or else have a stultifying surfeit of it.

A few days ago a friend gifted me a recent translation of Rainer Maria Rilke's *Sonnets to Orpheus*. Thanks to the lengthy introduction I again became acquainted with the life, loves and peregrinations across Europe of this prodigiously talented, soulful poet, whose amours knew no limits, from innocent freckled maidens to aging married countesses. He was clearly a charmer. Most of his life he survived only by the largesse of patrons, male or female. He developed rheumania and died at age fifty-one in a Swiss castle embracing a woman whose husband was out hunting with his dogs. Nonsense? Betcher bottom dollar.

It is easy enough to label Rilke as the quintessential puer, ever the footloose rascal, but become acquainted with his poetry and one cannot judge him harshly for all that. It is a common question: Do you evaluate artists by their lives or by what they produce? I am on the fence there, for I am as puer as they come.

You may recall the legend of the frog and the scorpion on the bank of a river. Here is a version by the jazz singer William Galison:

> One hot night in the middle of June
> In a Lousiana Bayou by the light of the moon
> By the bank of a river, on an old dead log
> Sat a shiny black scorpion and a big green frog
>
> Now the water was deep and the river was wide
> And the Scorpion had commitments on the opposite side
> She said Hey Mr Froggy I'd be mighty obliged
> If I could hop on your back and you could give me a ride
>
> Shoulda known
> Shoulda known
> Well my friends oh, see me crying
> And all they can say is shoulda known
>
> Well the frog said I'd love to but there's just one thing
> You got a bad reputation for a terrible sting
> If I take you cross the River like you're askin' me to
> How do I know you won't sting me when the journey is through?

The scorpion said "Man don't believe the hype. Don't you fall for that
tired old stereotype"
"If you do me this favor and deliver me there
I will tell you a little secret only scorpions share."

Shoulda known
Shoulda known
Well my friends oh see me crying
And all they can say is
Shoulda known

So our friends started out across the perilous flood
And the scorpion weighed more than the frog thought she would
But the froggy was strong and he knew he'd prevail
Til he felt the deadly point of that scorpion's tail

So the water swept over the unfortunate pair
And the froggy cried out with the last of his air
He said "Why did you do it?, now you're goin' down too!"
Said the Scorpion "It's my nature, that's what scorpions do."

And here is where it becomes personal.

You shoulda known
You shoulda known
Well my friends do see me crying
And all they can say is
You shoulda known, alright!

Well I met her downtown in a bleecker street bar
Serenading some drunks for the tips in a jar
Well I knew her reputation from the old grapevine
But she sounded so sweet and she looked so fine

Well she shot me a smile and she bought me a beer
And she told the saddest story that ever will hear
My judgement dissolved in a bottle wine
I was reading her lips and she was reading my mind

Shoulda known
I shoulda known
Well my friends oh see me crying
And all they can say is
Shoulda known

If the end of the story isn't perfectly plain
Know that Happy ever after ain't the final refrain
But my time's getting short and the story is long

But suffice it to say, you find me singin' this song

Shoulda known
I shoulda known
Well my friends do see me crying
And all they can say is
Shoulda known

Well my friends do see me crying
And all they can say is
Shoulda known.[38]

Now isn't that quite a cautionary tale? My erstwhile friend and colleague Arnold liked to refer to it when I scolded him for some supposed boyish stunt (like seducing our landlady in Zurich). "Well," he'd say, "You shoulda known. It's my nature; that's what puers do!"

*

I should confess here that in my early twenties I imagined emulating Rilke. This fanciful notion, improbably fostered by reading his *Notebook of Malte Laurids Brigge,* was overtaken when I fell in love with B, as recounted here earlier. I thereafter followed a somewhat erratic course in life, some of it at the behest of a greater power, but I am comfortable with where I am now. I only miss every love I (n)ever had.

There's a light
A certain kind of light
That never shone on me
I want my life to be lived with you
Lived with you
There's a way everybody say
To do each and every little thing
But what does it bring
If I ain't got you, ain't got?

You don't know what it's like, baby
You don't know what it's like
To love somebody

---

[38] "Shoulda Known," on William Galison and Madeleine Peyroux, *Got You On My Mind;* Ascap.

To love somebody
To love somebody
The way I love you.

In my brain
I see your face again
I know my frame of mind
You ain't got to be so blind
And I'm blind, so very blind
I'm a man, can't you see
What I am
I live and breathe for you
But what good does it do
If I ain't got you, ain't got?[39]

****

Fourteen
Miles from Nowhere

No wonder older men take up with twenty-something women. Young ladies seem to be innocent, naïve, still adventurous,, vivacious, inviting mentoring by a man of experience. Not to mention that they are sexually alive, whereas older women have often long since lost interest in such intimacy—around fifty their libido plummets; then their options are to take hormone replacement therapy, or lie back and think of England (or Ireland, Ethiopia, Mexico, Canada, wherever). Or, perhaps, find a new enlivening partner with whom to rediscover herself, as in the film *Shirley Valentine*. Life is an adventure, if you let it be, though of course it can cost more, in hindsight, than you care to pay.

---

[39] "To Love Somebody," Nina Simone, lyrics by Bee Gees; Ascap.

I am skating on thin ice here, for I know the reverse is also prevalent—frisky older women whose mates have lost interest except for fantasies in the coffee shop or on the golf course. Frustration is genderless. So is nonsense.

Personally, dare I say it, I prefer women closer to my own age, so at least the generation gap is not an issue.

7. There are not more than five musical notes, yet the combinations of these five give rise to more melodies than can ever be heard.
8. There are not more than three primary colors
   (blue, yellow, red, plus black and white), yet in combination
   they produce more hues than can ever been seen.
9. There are not more than five cardinal tastes
   (sour, acrid, salt, sweet, bitter), yet combinations
   of them yield more flavors than can ever be tasted.

Pardon me, but I don't recall where I found the above items. Maybe I just plucked them from the Pleroma.

*

Okay, back to business. In 1937 Jung gave a lecture in English at Yale University in New Haven, Connecticut, on the subject of religion in the light of science and philosophy. It was subsequently known as the "Terry Lecture" and later published in his *Collected Works* under the title "Psychology and Religion."

In this lecture, at a time when he was little known in America, Jung was at pains to explain his understanding of the unconscious and especially his hypothesis of the "autonomous complex," which he described as an association of ideas that could grip a person mercilessly, beyond reason, and was evidence that the mind could affect the body; that is, that some illnesses were psychosomatic.

As a case in point, he recounted the story of a patient who obsessively believed he had cancer. This man went to many doctors, who all pronounced him fit, but he persisted in his belief. Jung summed up his assessment like this:

71

We can never be sure that a new idea will not seize either upon ourselves or upon our neighbours. We know from modern as well as from ancient history that such ideas are often so strange, indeed so bizarre, that they fly in the face of reason. . . .

As a matter of fact, it only needs a neurosis to conjure up a force that cannot be dealt with by rational means. Our cancer case shows clearly how impotent man's reason and intellect are against the most palpable nonsense. I always advise my patients to take such obvious but invincible nonsense as the manifestation of a power and meaning they have not yet understood. Experience has taught me that it is much more effective to take these things seriously and then look for a suitable explanation. But an explanation is suitable only when it produces a hypothesis equal to the morbid effect. Out patient is confronted with a power of will and suggestion more than equal to anything his consciousness can put up against it. In this precarious situation, it would be bad strategy to convince him that in some incomprehensible way he is at the back of his own symptom, secretly inventing and supporting it. Such a suggestion would instantly paralyse his fighting spirit, and he would get demoralized. It is far better for him to understand that his complex is an autonomous power directed against his conscious personality. Moreover, such an explanation fits the actual facts much better than a reduction to personal motives. An apparently personal motivation does exist, but it is not made by his will, it just happens to him.[40]

Now, that's more nonsense than you could put in an elephant's trunk. I can hardly relate to it. It's true that I have chronically sore feet and my bowels hiss from time to time, but I've never been hyperchondriacal or cancer-obsessive. I do the blood-letting, -oscopies and chest x-rays regularly and monitor all the organs. My naturopathic-savvy doctor oversees my general health. I take milk thistle, DeepImmune and I suck lemons. I have a cardiologist and a neurosurgeon on my side, also a dermatologist and an eye doctor. All that costs me nothing. This is Canada, remember, where we have gummint-funded health care. I do pay for the lemons and my ace dentist, but he's affordable and I fancy his blonde assistant. I

---

[40] "Psychology and Religion," *Psychology and Religion,* CW 11, pars. 23, 26.

wear a lifeline button around my neck in case I should have a stroke or stumble and fall or get abducted again by aliens, but I eschew travel and illegal drugs. I'm not 100%, you understand, but I'm not aiming for longevity in the Guinness book. I'll be happy if I outlive my state-of-the-art iMac, Intel dual processor, 2GB storage, 2MG memory. Meanwhile I'm always grateful, and a little surprised, when I wake up to a new day.

I used to think so hard I thought my brain would explode. And finally it did, but benevolently. It hurtled me from thinking into the world of feeling, which is to say Eros and all the nonsense that goes with it. Not to say that thinking doesn't have its own nonsense to deal with, but that's a different story, quite as shadowy as mine.

Stare at the wall for awhile and talk yourself down to earth.

*

I had a talk today with my anima, Rachel as I call her.

"What about nonsense?" I asked.

"Well, suit yourself," she said, as enigmatic as usual.

*

"I can live with dying, but the thought of a lengthy, lingering illness really disturbs me."

That is the view of most of my elderly clients (and incidentally mine too). They have worked through their complexes and relationship problems and have a good degree of peace with themselves. They are ready, if not actually eager, to leave this world.

But what lies ahead? No one knows. Of course, there are psychics aplenty who claim to be able to establish contact with loved ones in the Beyond, but they are patently bogus and prey on the wishful thinking of those left behind. My late mentor Marie-Louise von Franz wrote an interesting book about this, *On Dreams and Death*. Her editor and translator (from the original German) summed up her lifetime of experience in this succinct paragraph:

> The unconscious archetypal symbolism of the soul's metapsychic transformation resembles both the symbolism of the process of transformation

upon or just before death *and* also the symbolism of the individuation process, as it is experienced intrapsychically during one's lifetime—for instance in analysis. It looks as if the process of psychic development and the acquisition of higher states of consciousness do not cease with the death of the body but continue after death—admittedly in a psychic-spiritual world which is beyond our rational consciousness. The post-mortal process of development of the unconscious psyche seems to be *part* of the process of individuation which occurs progressively in this life, consciously or unconsciously: *the completion of the inner psychic totality, the Self.*[41]

Now, that is a pretty hard act to follow, so I won't even try. I am devoted to the work of Dr. von Franz and I appreciate the open-ended observation that death is but the continuation of life in another form, but *the unknown is unknown*, and that is the bottom line, whatever your ego-opinion.

****

Fifteen
Halfway to Dawn

The interdependence that develops between partners—or codependence as psychologists call it—is fueled by the desire to do nothing that displeases the other. This commonly results in inhibiting the actions of both, as tunefully expressed in this old ballad:

> Sometimes I'm happy,
> Sometimes I'm blue.
> My disposition
> Depends on you.

---

[41] Marie-Louise von Franz, *On Dreams and Death: A Jungian Interpretation,* foreword by Emmanuel Kennedy-Xipolitas, p. xi.

I never mind
The rain from the sky
If I can find
The sun in your eyes.
Sometimes I love you,
Sometimes I hate you.
But when I hate you,
It's 'cause I love you.
That's how I am
So what can I do?
I'm happy when I'm with you.
~interlude~
Sometimes I love you,
Sometimes I hate you.
But when I hate you,
It's 'cause I love you.
That's how I am
So what can I do?
I'm happy when I'm with you.
I'm happy when I'm with you.[42]

Recall here that our primary focus is on individuation—becoming who you were meant to be. This may at times involve acting out your shadowy thoughts and wishes; well, your nonsense. It is difficult if not impossible to do this without wondering whether your mate would approve or disdain your actions. As long as you are identified with your mate, you are stuck in the quagmire of *participation mystique*—tied to his or her contrasexual side, anima or animus. Sorry, but this is rather more complicated than I have space here to expand upon. Suffice to say that loving an Other makes you vulnerable to betraying yourself.

*

I get up to lots of nonsense late at night, fueled by Scotch or isolation. I phone or Skype or email friends, former lovers, or just anyone I might connect with. I listen to jazz and write. I know that it's the love of Jung

---

42 "Sometimes I'm Happy," Nat King Cole; lyrics by V. Youmans, I. Caesar; Ascap.

that keeps me going, but sometimes I wonder what it's worth to others.

Never mind, I know what it's worth to me. Alchemically speaking, many years ago I was a piece of lead, a minion in the Western culture of consumerism. Now I have some sparkles of gold, but only because I chanced upon the writings of Carl Jung.[43] I am not a fan of communist teachings. I favor capitalism and democracy, in spite of their faults. The nonsense that went on between the USA and Russia in the so-called cold war period is well described fictionally by John Le Carré, Robert Ludlum and Tom Clancy. I'm just glad I wasn't old enough to be part of it.

*

The other day I stopped into a spa advertising an especially low price of $35 for a manicure and a pedicure. I was serviced by a cute young Vietnamese belle with braces on her teeth. I tipped her $10, so maybe I'm in love. Jeez, she could be anywhere between 12 and 25; in her gingham bib and tucker she looked like Dorothy/Judy in Kansas.

She was young enough to be my granddaughter. So I didn't think of penetrating her body; rather, I was immediately taken with the fantasy of suffusing her mind with my brilliance to the point of uncontrollable desire. That is what happens in some old movies—the man is cool, aloof, while the woman becomes besotted and finally in desperation throws herself at him, which of course he can't resist. And then the animus/anima nonsense goes full bore. Screen icons Spencer Tracey and Katherine Hepburn were especially good at depicting such dog and cat encounters.

Well, of course these are fantasies me and my shadow could well do without, however nonsensically frisky they make me feel. Anyway, there's no reason I couldn't invite her for a latte. I am more or less harmless during daylight hours in a café. And there is more than one way to mentor a fetching young lass. I may be a lustful old idjit, but I take too many showers to be a dirty old man.

So, that spa treatment was a week ago. Today I took a bouquet of carnations to the young belle.

---

[43] See my *Jung Uncorked,* Book Four, pp. 29ff.

"Pardon me," I said, "but you are so pretty and good at what you do, I brought these for you. Can you come out for coffee?"

She smiled but hardly blinked. "Thank you, but my mother does not let me leave the shop with strangers or customers."

I smiled and backed out, abashed, but left the flowers.

*

I am up late, again. But I often wonder if I get too much sleep anyway, since I read somewhere that seniors supposedly need less sleep than younger people. Well, that's just statistics. My experience is that I need more sleep than I used to. Look your doctor in the eye and say, "Fuck your bell curve. I am me. I'm always tired."

I live with opposites, as does anyone seriously involved with his or her psychological whereabouts. That is the curse and blessing of becoming conscious—keeping track of yourself. And always there is the primary question: Am I driven by ego-desire or directed by the Self? The former is narcissism, the latter individuation. There is a fine line between the two, often only discerned in retrospect, experientially, by trial and error.

Let me leave you with one of my favorite romantic standards, sung here by "Lady Day," aka "Lady of the Gardenias," Billie Holiday. Talk about projection!

> I fell in love with you
> first time I looked into
> Them there eyes
> You've got a certain li'l cute
> way of flirtin' with
> Them there eyes
> They make me feel happy
> They make me feel blue
> No stallin'
> I'm fallin'
> Going in a big way for sweet little you
> My heart is jumpin'
> Sure started somethin' with
> Them there eyes

You'd better watch them if you're wise
They sparkle
They bubble
They're gonna get you in a
whole lot of trouble
You're overworkin' them
There's danger lurkin' in
Them there eyes
Maybe you think I'm just flirtin'
Maybe you think I'm all lies
Just because I get
romantic when I gaze into
Them there eyes.[44]

*

I look in the mirror and I no longer fancy myself with a beard. On the other hand, I don't like having to shave every day either. So I am caught between a beard and a hard place. Talk about the opposites; they aren't just a concept; they are part and parcel of my daily nonsense.

Well, hair on my face, or not, is a minor conflict in the grand scheme of things—my life, the world, etc.

****

Sixteen
Coming Up from Down

Einstein's Dreams, a little snippet of a book by Alan Lightman, has captivated me. It purports to be a novel, but it is actually a fascinating, ex-

---

[44] "Them There Eyes," on *Billie's Blues"* (1942), lyrics by Maceo Pinkard, William Tracey, Doris Tauber; Ascap.

tended, philosophically intuitive foray—a prose/poem—into the nature and many possibilities of time.

One chapter begins: "Imagine a world in which there is no time. Only images."—inviting us to fasten on a childhood memory, our first love, a parental embrace, whatever, images that last forever.

Another: "Suppose time is a circle, bending back on itself. The world repeats itself, precisely, endlessly."—thought provoking but not necessarily miserable.

And another: "Consider a world in which cause and effect are erratic. Sometimes the first precedes the second, sometimes the second the first. Or perhaps cause lies forever in the past while effect in the future, but future and past are entwined." Well, that's more than I can get my mind around, which is probably the author's very point!

And that's not the half of it. There is little mention of Einstein or his ideas (other than the title), so the content is really an elaboration of Lightman's dreams, which doesn't make a bit of difference. Old Albert's sensibility and theory of relativity permeate the pages, wherein everything about time is believably presented as being possible, even probable.

The mind does reel at the idea of alternate time universes. *Einstein's Dreams* is a joy to read and stimulates a new perception of what we time-bound mortals take for granted as reality. I am intrigued to know more about the imaginative mind/writer behind it.

Alan Lightman teaches physics and writing at M.I.T. His book is a gem, little but not slight. Don't miss it if you can.

I wanted to tell you about this book in case you thought I was only interested in sex and nonsense. Not that I care very much about what you project onto me. And that's another thing about getting old. You don't have to give a damn about other people's opinions. You can hide away and be your own self without feeling guilty about it.

Of course, you also have to be cognoscent of relationships with friends and relatives, and it is very tacky to be gratuitously offensive. There is an ineluctable balance to be honored in the process of individuation: attention to oneself and to others, one's place in the wider community. It's a devilish balance that can keep you awake at night and dozing in the office during the day.

Enough said. Time for a song. How about this:

> Some old hotel room in Memphis
> I see the city through the rain
> I'm just chasing me my time
> And remembering some pain
> See there once was a boy
> And on the street he'd surely die
> But the nightbird took him in
> And she taught him how to fly
> See the nightbird softly fly
> Why does she fly alone?
> Is the moonlight just a flame for her memory?
> Now she's gone
> Two bit bars and honky tonks
> Any pleasure can be found
> You can get just what you want
> If you lay your money down
> And lonely sailors do their drinking
> My, my, my how the brave men do die
> And the nightbird sells her pleasures
> Bringing tears to my eyes
> See the nightbird softly fly
> Why does she fly alone
> Is the moonlight just a flame for her memory
> Now she's gone
> So I guess I'll go out walking
> Lord, let the rain keep falling down
> I guess I'll go chase some memories
> On the dark side of town
> See the nightbird softly fly
> Why does she fly alone
> Is the moonlight just a flame for her memory

Now she's gone .[45]

Seventeen
The Big Head

Multitasking may be the death of me, and possibly all of Western civilization.

I have just been tracking myself do about twenty things at once: write checks, read emails, compose emails, order supplies, prepare bank deposits, write a shopping list, take out the garbage, load the dishwasher, change light bulbs, have a shower, check batteries in smoke alarms, burn a CD, answer the phone, print a fax, load the printer, edit a manuscript, phone a friend, read Jung, do the laundry, write an essay, listen to music, on and on until I think I might go mad. I hardly stop for breath, and lunch is a stand-up sandwich in the kitchen. Dinner? Don't ask me, I'm too busy sleeping or trying to catch the day's market figures on the radio.

And I am just a small potatoes' businessman in the world of multitasking. I am a single gent. There are millions out there who have 9-5 jobs, do all of the above and have a family to love and play with, diapers to change, camping gear to pack, travel to arrange, etc. So how do people find the time to work on themselves, in or out of analysis? Where the time to record dreams, do something creative, or at least think about the possibilities? Our time and energy are limited. Something has to give. Our Western culture survives on a shaky edifice of millions running about in order to be "productive." What a chimera. Anchorites had a comparatively lush life atop their sky-high poles.

> How much do I love you?
> I'll tell you no lie.
> How deep is the ocean?
> How high is the sky?

---

45 "Nightbird," by Eva Cassidy on *Eva By Heart;* Ascap. [lyricsmania.com]

How many times a day do I think of you?
How many roses are sprinkled with dew?
How far would I travel
To be where you are?
How far is the journey
From here to a star?
And if I ever lost you,
How much would I cry?
How deep is the ocean?
How high is the sky?[46]

Good night. I am sorry that I can no longer burn the candle at both ends. It is a law of nature, a trade-off. The cost of staying up late with my nonsense is losing the morning hours. So be it, according to what is right in front of me, as I have always functioned. Well, tomorrow is another day, or possibly oblivion. I favor the former, but I am ready for either.

****

Eighteen
Once in a While

I don't like going to the computer after dinner without an exit strategy. After cleaning up the emails I am apt to get hooked into the music and fine-tuning this manuscript, and before I know it it's 4 a.m. Funny how time flies when you're having fun. (It's better than a roller coaster, even a Ferris Wheel.) Then, barring early appointments, I am bound to sleep till noon.

Of course I love dancin' with the muse and skirtin' the blues into the wee hours, but I don't like feeling wasted the next day and missing the

---

[46] "How High Is the Sky?" lyrics by Irving Berlin, 1932; Ascap.

early hours of the morning when it is easier to get work done without interruptions by phone or fax.

On the other hand, it can be very disheartening being up from 8 a.m. until midnight trying to write a book.

The opposites again. It's like I said earlier about the facial hair I sport: caught between a beard and a hard place.

All that is true, well and good, but remember, I'm not in charge. To stay on my path, I may sometimes be obliged to play second fiddle to a higher authority. Still, I generally set a time limit to my nonsense—say midnight, more or less, but often more, carried away by life.

*

I have a neighbor who often passes by, swinging her long legs and grocery bags, smiling at me.

This neighbor stops once in a while to chat on my doorstep. She is not a spring chicken and not overtly provocative, but she has a mystical, vulnerable smile that does hook me. Just my type, and beyond child-bearing years, barring immaculate conception. Her name is Peggy Sue, honest. Come back to the Five and Dime, I think, though I'm no Jimmy Dean. I am quite taken with her, for no apparent reason.

I imagine inviting her in for a drink.

In the kitchen she says, "I'll have what you're having." Which happens to be Scotch choked with ice. My buddy. I put Fleetwood Mac on the stereo.

"Peggy Sue," I say, "do you realize that I'm attracted to you?"

"I've heard that before," she replies, "but never from a fella so charming and learnèd—mostly from the jackasses I used to work with at the bank."

I shrug. "I bin just an ordinary guy who fancies you. How do you feel about that?"

She laughs. "It's fine with me, but the last palooka who came on to me wasn't very popular with my husband, who put him in the hospital for a month."

Yeah, that figures. I knew he'd been a ranked welterweight.

"Peggy Sue," I say, "let's not get ahead of ourselves. All I'd like now is to hold you, maybe dance a little."

"I don't care much for smoking."

"I'll stop."

"I got a beard at home and it irritates my skin."

"I'll take it off."

"Your eyebrows are kinda curly."

"I'll trim them."

She smiles and pulls me close. Her breasts are small, pointy under a thin pink shift; being near them makes me crazy. And her pudendum?— well, don't ask.

"I really like your tits," I say.

PS laughs, "Oh, I like crude, say it again."

I do and she eyes me, hiking her skirt. No undies; well, it's a hot summer day. I am so erect I could polevault.

"I gotta pistola here," she says, "that ain't been fired in months, cowboy, so gimme what you got."

About then I realize that I am acting out a Harlequin romance and I step back. My cold feet stop dancing.

"Peggy Sue," I say, "sorry, but I can't do this. I'm a studious writer who has no business romancing a married woman whose husband was a prizefighter. Not your fault, honest. Maybe we could play Scrabble or read Rilke together."

PS puts herself back together and glares at me. "I'm sorry too. I thought we had something going, but you're just a chickenshit. I got one of them at home and I don't need another."

She blows me a kiss as she leaves. It is way more than I deserve for my smoke and mirrors nonsense.

2:15 a.m. Pulling myself away from Miles Davis trumpeting the score of *Porgy and Bess,* I fall into bed.

****

Nineteen
Pick Up Sticks

I believe that making love is an acquired art, especially if you fell asleep during anatomy class.

Denise, my very first sweetheart as a teenager in Ottawa, taught me a lot about pleasuring a woman. She was a cheerleader; she dove and swam like a mermaid and had a curvaceous body like Esther Williams. We were both seventeen. We petted in my father's 1948 DeSoto, 4 cylinder, stick shift, fluid drive. I was clumsy; she was not shy.

"Yes," she'd say, "a little up, to my left, oh do it harder!"

She left me for Paul Anka. I wasn't very sore; I liked his singing too. But I sure missed her warm body. My shadow stalked her for a few days before I got over it. John Lennon sang the feeling years later to his enigmatic and frisky soul mate, Yoko Ono:

> I was dreaming of the past.
> And my heart was beating fast,
> I began to lose control,
> I began to lose control,
>
> I didn't mean to hurt you,
> I'm sorry that I made you cry,
> I didn't want to hurt you,
> I'm just a jealous guy,
>
> I was feeling insecure,
> You night not love me any more,
>
> I was shivering inside,
> I was shivering inside,
>
> I was trying to catch your eyes,
> Thought that you were trying to hide,
> I was swallowing my pain,

I was swallowing my pain.[47]

I sometimes fall asleep counting not sheep but the women I've coupled with, or wanted to. In my sleep-daze I fasten not on quantity but on quality. Truth to tell, it wasn't until I was in my thirties that I realized where things were and what to do with them. Everything before that was mechanical, and I was naïve enough to think that a woman who enjoyed a flirtatious dance was interested in making love. More, I didn't know the difference between an erection and Eros until I was about forty. And a woman's G-spot was never talked about in the mid-twentieth century.

There is an enormous difference for a man between seeing a woman as a sex object and as someone to relate to. Of course, I still see women instinctively as objects of desire, but I have learned to pay attention also to who they are, who is behind, say, a fashionably-clothed façade. Oh, she is a person too! I have learned to consider their needs and wants, their psychology, and also my projections. This does severely limit my potential field of conquest, and inhibits my reputation as a rake-hell, but on the whole it has kept me out of trouble, if not clear of nonsense.

Such a development does not come naturally to men, especially those who are more used to thinking than feeling. The meaning of relatedness/Eros has to be learned experientially over many years and through contact with many women, one heartache after another—starting with loss of the mother. In the terms of analytical psychology, it is a man's inner woman, his anima, who absorbs his experience and informs his ego-attitude toward women in the outside world. Mind you, she does this in service to the Self, who is after all in charge of re-establishing contact with who one is essentially meant to be.

I dare to say that something similar can happen for women, in which case it is their inner man, or animus, who helps them graduate from desire for a body or a father-surrogate to appreciation of a particular man—and thereby differentiate sex from Eros.

Many relationships thrive on the differentiation between desire and Eros; others may fail for lack of it. Whatever, stay together or part ways,

---

[47] "Jealous Guy," Lyrics by Lennon, on *Imagine* (1971); Ascap. Watch it on YouTube.

the consequences depend on the psychological sophistication of the partners—acrimony and Eros are antinomies.

Making love invariably complicates a relationship, but repressed desire can do even more damage. I have a lot more to say about relationships, but I have already said it more than once elsewhere,[48] so I'm going to bed now, and fare thee well with a song from my heart:

> I am a child, I'll last a while.
> You can't conceive of the pleasure in my smile.
> You hold my hand, rough up my hair,
> It's lots of fun to have you there.
> God gave to you, now, you give to me,
> I'd like to know what you learned.
> The sky is blue and so is the sea.
> What is the color, when black is burned? What is the color?
> You are a man, you understand.
> You pick me up and you lay me down again.
> You make the rules, you say what's fair,
> It's lots of fun to have you there.
> God gave to you, now, you give to me,
> I'd like to know what you learned.
> The sky is blue and so is the sea.
> What is the color, when black is burned? What is the color?
> I am a child, I'll last a while.
> You can't conceive of the pleasure in my smile.[49]

*

I am hard-wired to adore women, perhaps because of my father's oft-professed love for my mother. Anyway, that and my mother's carefully attuned Eros resulted in my having a so-called positive mother complex, which is both good and bad.

Recall that any complex is an accretion of associations around a particular idea or theme. All my early experience of "mother" and female

---

[48] See, for instance, my books *Jungian Psychology Unplugged: My Life As an Elephant*, pp. 70ff., and *Digesting Jung: Food for the Journey*, pp. 67ff.

[49] "I am a Child," lyrics by Neil Young; Ascap.

teachers and relatives was wonderfully self-affirming. I thrived in the limelight of their affection and encouragement. I was clean-cut, smart as a whip, always top of the class, and I moved confidently into the outside world to make my mark. And I did, thanks to the recruiters from Procter & Gamble, who pegged me as just their kind of guy. And I was, at that time. They flew me down to Cincinnati to meet the top brass and gave me a key to the corporate washroom. They paid me well, gave me a room with my name on the door, a personal secretary, cameras and a position as Director of Public Relations, Canada. I became editor of their in-house magazine, *Moonbeams.* I was just twenty-two, and already a junior executive. I took everything at face-value. Now, talk about inflation, and think about peacocks. Girlfriends? I was swarmed by pudenda.

And that's where the other side of the mother complex comes in. I was easily seduced by appearances. I could never think ill of any woman, always vulnerable to a lover's dark side (animus/shadow). But as I learned much later in life, there is a shadow side to everything and every one—something behind the scenes that you may be only dimly aware of until it hits you in the face.

What hit me in the face in 1959 was the meaninglessness of what I was doing, however much I was enjoying my cushy, semi-fraudulent job day-to-day. All the letters of complaint came to me. There were a lot. I would lean back in my pumped-up $800 swivel chair, feet on the desk, and dictate answers.

My secretary was named Gladys—buxom, buck toothed and perky, with a silver button in one ear.

"Dear Gladys, take a letter." And she'd open her pad and transcribe my words in the long-lost art of shorthand.

"Dear Mr. Bell, comma, new paragraph. Thank you for your recent letter, period. We are most surprised to learn that unlike many thousands of satisfied Whitey Toothpaste users, comma, your teeth have turned black, period. Although laboratory tests have proved the Whitey white-ness claims, comma, it is just possible that in your case the effect may not be as immediate as with others, period. Or as bad."

Gladys giggled. Dear Gladys, she thought I was a hoot.

"New paragraph. Ahhh, nevertheless, comma, true to our promise, we herewith refund your money plus postage and two free giant-size Whiteys, period. We hope that you will persevere, comma, proving for yourself that Whitey Toothpaste really does make teeth whiter, period. Yours sincerely, etc."

"Gladys, there are more of those. Send a copy to Quality Control, with a memo—whose teeth are you using down there?"

"Say Gladys, where's that report on skin eruptions? Cal Dave Stephens at the *Telegram*. Tell him I've been called away on important business. Tell him, uh, the company's lawyers are looking into these complaints with a view to settling out of court in case their truth in substance is established, which we do not of course admit.

"Send another memo to Quality Control—What are you doing to the Bunny Flakes? The old man is on to this. It could be your skin next."

"Gladys, take a letter.

"Dear Mr. Appleby. We are sorry indeed to hear of the distress you experienced through the use of our product, comma, Mother Maxwell's Quick-Make Bicky-Mix, period. I assure you it is not usual to find a mouse in it, period. Our Bicky-Mix foreman attributes this to the playful antics of some of our more junior employees, comma, who will nevertheless be duly disciplined, period.

"New paragraph. Mr. Appleby, comma, under separate cover we are sending you one dozen packs of Mother Maxwell's Quick-Make Bicky-Mix, comma, of assorted kinds, period. We hope you will continue to inform us of any irregularities in our products that come to your attention, period. Quality Control, comma, Mr. Appleby comma, is an everyday concern here, period. Yours etc."

That's the way it went. Sand in the talcum powder, mice in the cake mix, hair in the jam. Gladys would punch out the letters on a tape and run off a few dozen copies on an electric typewriter that made them look individually typed. That was part of the game. I didn't think twice about it. Bound to be some problems in a company that size. Somebody had to answer the letters, and I was paid handsomely to do just that.

They said I had the right stuff and would quickly move up through the ranks. I lived in a large bachelor flat with modern furniture and a state-of-the-art hi-fi. I had a two-year-old Dodge and a hand-made suit that cost $250. I looked quite impressive in midnight blue. I had my hair cut every Thursday and used Wild Root Cream-Oil to keep it neat. On payday I had a shoeshine for a quarter. "Here," I'd say, handing over three dimes, "keep the change."

I was captain of the bowling team. I had three cameras. I took pictures of factory workers and edited *Moonbeams*. After work I played softball and drank beer with the boys.

I was doing what my education had prepared me for. Others of my age were climbing mountains, exploring jungles, roaming around the world. I didn't envy them. Why would I? They were shirking the duties of real life. They had no place in society; I was a valuable team member in the business community.

I was an organization man and I liked it. Fun? A bushel and a peck.

However, after two years of such nonsense I became uneasy and restless. My bowling average dropped. On the diamond I couldn't pitch for beans. I had a bad case of itchy feet.

In 1958 it finally came down to a choice between a 1956 Thunderbird convertible with the thousand dollars I'd saved, or going to Europe. A thousand bucks went a long way in those days.

For a few weeks it was a toss-up, but in the end I opted for the Old World. And that's how I became a struggling writer with nothing to say. I still had not heard of Jung, but when I did I rejoiced in his injunction to "follow your energy." Robert Frost said it like this:

> Two roads diverged in a yellow wood.
> And sorry I could not travel both
> And be one traveler, long I stood
> And looked down one as far as I could
> To where it bent in the undergrowth;
>
> Then took the other, as just as fair,
> And having perhaps the better claim,
> Because it was grassy and wanted wear;
> Though as for that the passing there

Had worn them really about the same.

And both that morning equally lay
In leaves no step had trodden black.
Oh, I kept the first for another day!
Yet knowing how way leads on to way,
I doubted if I should ever come back.

I shall be telling this with a sigh
Somewhere ages and ages hence:
Two roads diverged in a wood, and I—
I took the one less traveled by,
And that has made all the difference.[50]

The rest is my history, which I have recounted here earlier and elsewhere at more length.[51]

****

Twenty
Fare Thee Well

Okay, let's talk about projection. I am moved to discuss this because of
an email from a close friend yesterday:

> I am desperate for your help! How does one know what projection means?
> Is life meaningful? If so, do we live life through projection, or do we live
> life blindly . . . and if it's projection, and we know it, how is that meaning-
> ful? Please enlighten me.

Jeez, these are valid but heavy questions, virtually unanswerable without some context. This man has read my books, so he knows the theory;
now he wants to hear it from the guru's mouth (itself a projection, since I
am no guru). I could only guess that his relationship with his wife of

---

[50] "The Road Not Taken," in *Mountain Interval.*

[51] Notably in *The Survival Papers* and *Dear Gladys.*

some six years had hit a snag.

What am I to do or say? I am quite in the dark about how to respond. I am particularly fond of this man, and I have invited him to talk about it in person, but meanwhile, in order not to project my own self onto him, let me step away from the actual situation and rehearse what I would say to any client, call him Ishmael.

Simply said, when our expectations of others are frustrated or thwarted, you can be sure that projection is involved. In many cases it is aspects of ourselves that we unwittingly see, or wish to see, in the other. Or it may be our experience of a parent we project onto the other. Projection is not an act of will; we don't do it deliberately, it just happens. And when others thwart our desires, we have an opportunity to withdraw our projections. That is when life becomes as meaningful as you want to make it, because consciousness changes everything. Relationships founder because one refuses to see the reality of the other. They can thrive when projections are withdrawn.

Me: Can you tell me how you came to ask these questions? What is going on in your life?

Ishmael: It's Daisy Mae—she has withdrawn from me. She's not who she used to be. We were always so close. Now she wants this, I want that, and there's no in-between. She says I'm not the man she married.

Me: Well, maybe she's still herself, but just not who you thought she was. Maybe she hid herself behind a bushel in order to please you. And maybe you did the same to please her.

Ishmael: Well, she is a good mother to Simon, but hardly gives me the time of day. Now, why would I stay with her when she isn't who I thought she was?

Me: Good question, but one you can't sort out by thinking about it. How do you feel about her? Do you love her? Is there still a passionate connection? What would you do without her? Does she want to work this out together? Life may call you to different paths.

I went through some of the above with my friend when we were together, and ended up suggesting he have a few sessions with a colleague. We were much too close for me to counsel him myself.

****

Twenty-One
Punching Air

I was a dedicated smoker, rolling my own, for almost fifty years until I quit cold turkey six years ago. It wasn't difficult; I had no withdrawal symptoms to speak of.

Foolishly, some two years ago, prompted by a traumatic experience, I began smoking again, still rolling my own. Now I would like to stop, but I am not finding it so easy this time. I have cut back, but the craving, the habit, persists. I hate tailor-mades. The brand name of the tobacco I roll into cigarettes is Drum, made in the Netherlands and sold all over the world. Every pouch carries a warning from Health Canada; for instance: "Cigarettes are Highly Addictive. Studies have shown that tobacco can be harder to quit than heroine or cocaine."

I can believe it. I think of Frank Sinatra as a junkie in *The Man With a Golden Arm,* and Gene Hackman in *The French Connection.* If they could beat heroine, and they did, then I betcha I can stop smoking. To this end I decided to bring to bear the time-honored Jungian method of dialoguing with a complex, which is what I dub it on account of my intellectual infrastructure. (Others may call it the devil, Lucifer, or simply a "bad habit.") Personifying a complex is a way of re-educating the brain, so to speak. In this case I call my vis-à-vis Mr. Tobah Ko (TK).

TK: Hey there Doc, I was sleeping. What's up?

Me: Mr. Tobah Ko, you are a handsome fella in your blue and red wrapper, but I am fed up with you. You give me phlegm, you make me cough and leave me breathless. Also, you are a very expensive companion.

TK: Hey, give me a break. You're a half-empty kind of guy. Look on the half-full side of it. I am your best friend in the deep of the night, We both love jazz and Scotch. I give you inspiration. I put words in your mouth.

Me: Get away with you. You smile but bin a villain. You put a bad taste in my mouth. You are an evil-smelling blackguard, a disgusting blood-sucker. I wrote several books without missing you, never gave you a thought.

TK: Were they as good as when we were together?

Me: Not for me to say. But it's enough for me to know that I don't need you in order to express myself. And worst of all, my health suffers when you're around. My lungs work overtime to clear themselves of your noxious fumes. My arteries clog up. My toes tingle. My feet are sore. My ears whistle. In short, I have stopped enjoying you.

TK: I love you. We are a great team. We've had many good times together.

Me: Yes, we've been close, that's for sure. I have loved you like a brother and enjoyed the rolling ritual, but no more. Listen to what's in you (reading from the pouch): tar, nicotine, carbon monoxide, formaldehyde, hydrogen cyanide, benzene, and more. I mean, *hydrogen cyanide!* That's what they use in pesticides to exterminate rats and other vermin! And formaldehyde is used to preserve dead bodies! Benzene is demonstrably carcinogenic and long-term exposure at various levels can affect normal blood production and can be harmful to the immune system. It can cause leukemia and has also been linked to heart attacks, strokes, birth defects in animals and humans. God love a duck, you're a friggin' time-bomb! You turn life into smoke. You're all style—smoke and mirrors—an illusion of the good life. You make my lungs black and sticky and icky. If you really cared for me, you would not tempt me to roll another.

TK: You make some points, but I gotta see some data before goin' into underdrive. My paymasters, the cigarette-manufacturing titans, will never back down, no matter the evidence. You see, there are so many jobs at stake, including mine. The tobacco titans will obscure the daily reality until they have no dollars left to defend themselves— but don't hold your breath, for they have deep pockets and friends in high places.

Between you and me, that's always been the problem. I tried to get them to clean me up, but they just laughed. I am teamed with many others who have families, and your views will destroy them.

ME: Cry me a river, crocodile tears. The beating of my heart is more important that the beating of a drum. It's crazy to put your poisons into a human body, and so far I'm sane, so fare thee well, you parasitic rascal. Behind your seductive façade you bin simply an antisocial, unhealthy habit, and I will have no more of you. Take this personally. You are not my best friend; you're my worst enemy. Go find yourself another sucker to make a living. Redrum is murder spelled backwards. Get away with ya!

TK fades away.......... and I go back to reading *Allen Carr's Easy Way to Stop Smoking.*

Rachel suddenly manifests. "You idjit, come out of the corner and take off that silly dunce cap! Come now, pull yourself together. You're an analyst. When you come to your senses, join me for a little slap and tickle in the Pleroma."

*

That ought to hold TK (and me) for tonight, and I can hope that soon I'll have a Drumless day. I am wiped out. Demon fighting takes energy! It would probably be easier with a warm and willing mate, but I mustn't think that way; loneliness is just an excuse to Drum another.

****

Twenty-Two
Black Turnip

I can, under duress, invent scenarios, but I would hesitate to call my writing creative. My shadow does all the work; viz. this vignette:

"You're an attractive woman. What would you like me to know about you?"

Hardly the most original approach to a hot blonde on a stool beside you in the Bar Italia on College Street , but it won me a smile.

"In short," she said, "bugger all."

"Hey," I replied, "I'm quite harmless."

"That's what I was afraid of," she said.

She eyed me up and down. "The truth is, most guys who come on to me are barely out of diapers. I bin over eighteen and I rather favor older men," she said.

I touched her hand. "Lucky me. I bin forty-two and fancy younger women."

She laughed. "You bin fulla shit. With that beard you bin as ancient as days, like you just stepped out of a William Blake engraving."

Me (thinking): Oh, she's literate, that's a bonus.

She asks, "What's your handle?"

"I'm Razr," I said, "and you?"

"You can call me Jezebel," she replied with a shrug, "and I bet I'm almost as old as you."

Okay, so she wasn't twenty-five, and I wasn't forty-two. These facts didn't trouble me or her, as it turned out.

Patti Page was blasting in the background, something about Tennessee. I said to Jezebel, "Do you dance?"

She upped off the stool and took my hand. "Whenever possible."

We waltzed around a very small space. She pulled me close. "You got unusual moves," she said.

I blushed. "You bring the high school out of me."

Jezebel attacked me with her pudendum. "Take me home," she said.

I lay down my arms. "Your place or mine?"

She laughed, "You're so full of clichés and Old Spice, it's charming. Come on, I live just around the corner."

I paid the tab and we bolted out a side door into an alley, where she thrust herself against me. That felt good. It was raining. That felt bad.

But Jezebel unfolded a portable umbrella to shield us from the worst.

She then led me on a two-minute walk to her apartment, a second-floor unit above a paint supply store.

"You better take off your duds, buddy," she said, doffing hers. "You bin wet to the bone. Swine flu is everywhere."

Well, she was even more attractive without clothes. My blood raced to catch up with my mind.

"Do you give hugs on a first date?" I asked.

"Try me," she replied. I did and she did.

"Like a drink?" she asked.

"Scotch, if you have any, lotsa ice."

Jezebel poured us each a healthy tumbler. "What do you do for a living?" she asked.

I said, "As little as possible. I inherited wealth from an uncle who had a widget factory. He stole from Peter and paid Paul almost nothing. In my spare time I write books about nonsense. When I run out of ideas I go out looking for someone to frolic with."

"Suits me," said Jezebel. "I bin a secretary in a funeral home. I seen enough dying to creep me out into living."

It was a small apartment. You could hardly move without falling into her queen-sized bed, which we did rather quickly. She was on top of me. We kissed. My spine tingled. I wasn't erectile dysfunctional.

I held her away. "I should tell you, I am betrothed to another."

Jezebel lowered herself onto me. "So am I. But that's tomorrow. Let's make the most of today."

To desire and be desired may be the closest we can come to feeling like gods. And yes, it may be projection and it may not last, but live your nonsense, for it is the stuff of your life..

We fell asleep nestled in each other's arms.

I think I heard her say, "I like making love for the sheer joy of it. Thank you for being here."

Now that's a common attitude for a man, but among women it is as rare as fur on fish.

****

Twenty-Three
Bumpin' on Sunset

"I just wish they'd leave me alone to play with my stones."

I've always treasured that metaphor, spoken by a true artist: Jerry Pethick, Canadian-born sculptor (1935-2003), when his mentors at the Royal Academy of Art in London, England called his work into question. His student-peers were the likes of David Hockney, Frank Bowling and others who subsequently soared to fame.

Jerry courted fame erratically, with many showings in New York, Japan, Europe and most public galleries in Canada. He won much respect from his peers. Had he garnered fortune he would have given it away to the first indigent street-corner musician. He and his wife Margaret lived on a shoestring in England, Detroit, San Francisco, and finally on Hornby Island in British Columbia. He had friends like me who sometimes paid the way, collecting his works because we loved his attitude, his ethics, his art, and just being in his presence. He was such fun to be with, playful and alert and always intuitively creative. He could turn a napkin into a work of art. He wasn't a womanizer, but he would chase anything that sparked his imagination. He virtually invented holography as an art form (and I published his little book on it).[52]

I recall a time he came to visit me in Toronto with a dozen small cartoon drawings that I bought for a trifling or handsome sum, I forget which. (He never took advantage of my willingness to buy; always asked a bargain price for the best pieces to fit into my collection.) Then we spent a whole day driving around the city looking for frames. We finally found some suitable ones in a dollar store and rejoiced after in the Horseshoe Tavern, one of our favorite Toronto haunts in those days when we weren't playing snooker.

---

[52] *On Holography and a Way to Make Holograms.*

Jerry Pethick was a phenomenon of nature. He never doubted who he was, never questioned his destiny, his talent, his vocation, his essence. He was born and grew up in London, Ontario, where he spent two years at the University of Western Ontario, with summers working in the Sudbury nickel mines, before his restless spirit called him to London, England. In 1957 he became a student at the Chelsea Polytechnic School of Art, receiving a diploma in 1960. He went on to graduate with honors from the Royal College of Art in 1964, along with other notables.

I met Jerry in a London pub in 1959. That pub was the legendary Finch's on the Fulham Road. The publican was a big-hearted Irishman, Jack Connell, who remained a close friend of Jerry's over the many years after. Finch's was like a home away from home for many ex-patriot Canadians in the 50s and 60s. We gathered there to meet and drink and make Mary merry. We were struggling painters and sculptors and writers, pretty full of ourselves. We worked hard at our individual crafts and then we played our young hearts out at Finch's, the Queen's Elms and other establishments of questionable repute. Some of us actually went on to make a name for ourselves as artists of one kind or another. Others grew out of what was just a passing phase and became stockbrokers, advertising executives, journalists, etc. In the long run, you fished or cut bait.

In that milieu—the Canadian so-called ex-pat artistic community—Jerry was a central figure. Physically large and strong, he was altogether bigger than life, an earthy charmer, a great talker and loyal friend, dedicated to pursuing his art, come what may. He was charismatic and didn't know it. He winkled his way into people's hearts. He pied-pipered his way through life. His salty humor, wide-ranging mind and open-hearted warmth endeared him to just about everyone. He was an altogether engaging rascal who in those early days had a huge appetite for carousing. His nocturnal exploits became almost mythical, like the time he crashed a casino with ten quid in his pocket and left with a thousand pounds Sterling, and then there was a painful midnight plunge through a skylight while seeking to tryst and shout. That time he took thirty stitches and just went back to work at his Chelsea garage job the next morning.

Jerry settled down, more or less, when he became enamoured of his future wife, Margaret, daughter of a banker. Margaret brooked no extramural nonsense, but her devotion to Jerry and support of his vocation knew few bounds. She tamed but did not change him. She graced and embraced his adventurous life for almost forty years, and in sickness, when he was immobilized with a brain tumor, cared for him to the end.

In the late sixties Jerry and Margaret moved to Ann Arbor, Michigan, where he pioneered in the practical applications of holography and its potential as an art form. He had a patent on his process, but he gave it up as bail for a friend who was busted for possession. They moved to San Francisco in 1972, where aging hippies like me visited them and blew our stoned minds in their living room listening to Janis Joplin, James Taylor, Crosby Stills & Nash and others on headphones. Jerry tolerated us and went on with his work in a warehouse loft.

Due to circumstances too bizarre to detail here, Jerry and Margaret turned up on Hornby Island, British Columbia, in 1975 with their infant son Yana—named after a native tribe in California. They lived in a cave for six months before Jerry built them a permanent home with windows and a loo. Their first house burned down due to an electrical fault. They lived with friends while Jerry built another. Hornby Island was thereafter their base, but for two or three months a year they would travel: to Toronto, back to England, Ireland, Paris, Vienna, Yugoslavia. Both gregarious, they had, and have, friends all over the world.

Over some forty years, Jerry Pethick became an internationally renowned artist, prolific and endlessly inventive. He received several Canada Council senior artist grants. His intriguing works are in many private homes as well as public galleries around the world, including Tokyo, Paris, London, Seattle, Toronto, Victoria, Ottawa and Vancouver. Just recently, many of his wall-pieces, or "drawings," were exhibited in a traveling show that started in Kamloops, B.C., and moved across Canada to Halifax, Rimouski and Toronto. My own house is a kaleidoscope of colorful Pethick works, featuring pieces with such evocative names as the Krieghoff Glass Book, Traversing the Void, Eskimo Snow-Glasses, Moon-Landing Foot-Pad, Pursuing the Eons, Dancing Penguin-

Propellors, and so on.

In recent years, embracing a long-standing interest in optical phenomena and technological processes, Jerry was concerned with virtual space as a sculptural medium. He was comfortable using diverse materials such as bottles, hand-blown glass, plastics, light bulbs, mirrors, Fresnel lenses, image-projecting devices, spectrafoil, photographs, as well as more traditional sculptural elements both made and found.

Bob Rodgers, a mutual friend, has written of Jerry's art: "He had an uncanny eye for seeing through the trash of our time–rusting metal, abandoned stoves and refrigerators, dinky toys, wastelands of superfluous electronics, abandoned plastics, gimmicks and gee-gaws from the superstores. Out of such ugliness, as if something human resided in them, he made works of astonishing elegance."

I can echo that.

Two years before his death Jerry entered a competition sponsored by the Vancouver development firm Concord Pacific to produce an outdoor work of art for a housing complex. (It is a little known fact that in Ontario and British Columbia, 1% of the cost of developing a commercial site must be spent on art.) Jerry's winning submission featured a giant cast-iron "time-top," slated to be immersed in water until it was barnacle encrusted—about two and a half years. Jerry finished all the planning and detailed drawings for this project, and Margaret saw it to completion after he was gone. I was there for the quai-side unveiling in 2005, along with about a thousand other fans and friends; it was a real blast—I fell down a few times and still have the bruises to show for it.

Jerry had an engaging, childlike curiosity. He was the cat's pyjamas, and also the cat. He was always making something out of something, as often as not something shrewdly constructed from objects picked up at the Hornby Island Recycling Center. And the hundreds of somethings he made, from his giant eight-foot high bottle man comprised of 425 varicoloured wine bottles, to his version of the Willendorf Venus (368 light bulbs), always had meaning. In an interview, he said: "I like the entertainment value of ideas when I'm working. It keeps me alive while I'm doing the work, so the work stays alive. It's got to be not boring to me or it's going to be boring to everybody else."

Jerry himself was never boring. He could be irritating and try your patience by talking your ear off when he got on a hobby-horse (complex) of one kind or another, but he was never boring. Personally, he enlivened me, and not only by his presence. Anticipating his coming put me on edge, bugled me to be ready for the unexpected. He could always jolly me out of a morose mood, and he was seldom in one himself that an hour or two in McVee's or the Horseshoe Tavern in Toronto—or an Irish pub anywhere—wouldn't dispell.

I do not generally favor the unknown. I am rather introverted and con-servative by nature. Jerry was anything but. And so, he personified a radical other side of me that came out to play when he was around. (Call it my shadow, why not.) When Jerry was nearby, I was under his spell. He vibrated possibilities. There was a sense that anything could happen, and often it did. I dropped everything to play snooker with him or drive the streets seeking arcane bits and pieces in hardware stores or junk shops—things he needed for one artwork or another (his orphans, as he called them, because they had no homes). We often searched in vain, though joyfully all the same, stopping every hour or so in a pub to wet our whistles and talk about art and sealing wax. Jerry embodied both nonsense and Eros. Thanks to him, I learned not to be overly goal-oriented, but rather to enjoy the process—the getting around, around, around . . .

I have used images of Jerry's artwork on the covers of several of the books I've written or published. The content of these books—the practi-cal application of Jungian psychology—was of little interest to him. But he always liked to hear why I did what I did, as I did about him and his work, and that was the strongest bond between us. We accepted each other's passion and played snooker whenever possible.

Jerry Pethick was an iconic personality in the art world of his time. He died in 2003, aged 67, sorely missed. A dozen friends and son Yana dug his grave on Hornby and buried him with honors.

I have about sixty of his unique orphans that I am bequeathing to the Art Gallery and Museum of London, Ontario.

It is so hard to stop the nonsense with the decibels bombarding your ears. Just now it's Keith Jarrett's haunting piano classic, *The Köln Concert,* a performance that catapulted jazz into the mainstream in 1975.

Well, tomorrow is another day.

Staying up into the wee hours is an indulgence, but on the other hand I often think I get too much sleep anyway; nine or ten hours at night and a two-hour nap add up. The opposites again.

See you anon-sense.

*

An elderly woman from Jamaica once said to me: "You get born, you grow up and have babies; they grow up and leave you with a husband who treats you like a potato. You washes clothes and dishes and then you die. I think I might better jump offa bridge."

Talk about bleak. But I could not gainsay her experience. What did I know? Anyway, soon after that session she dreamed:

> I am sailing, I am sailing, far across the sea. Then I am flying, I am flying, high up in the air. I see the Earth below and am glad to be alive.

You see, I didn't have to try to pull her out of her enmired negativity. Her own unconscious presented a compensating image.

Likewise, from time to time I am assailed by the thought that I am a bigger twit than anyone else. I know nothing, have nothing to say. In my profession this is what we call negative inflation. It is just part and parcel of a cyclic turn of events, like when I feel at the top of my craft I am simultaneously tormented by doubts. The technical term, psychologically, is *enantiodromia*—go to an extreme in one direction and the opposite will manifest to maintain a psychic balance.

Not a big deal. You live to writhe another day.

> What a day this has been
> What a rare mood I'm in
> Why, it's almost like being in love
> There's a smile on my face
> For the whole human race

Why, its almost like being in love
All the music of life seems to be
Like a bell that is ringing for me
And from the way that I feel
When that bell starts to peal
I would swear I was falling
I could swear I was falling
It's almost like being in love.[53]

****

Twenty-Four
Into the Mystic

I have a wonderfully close female friend. We are not sexually intimate. We like it that way—Eros but not overtly erotic. From time to time we boogy in the kitchen or the pool, but it doesn't lead to bed. Our relationship is chimerical, by which I mean I can project onto her anything I want, and she takes it in good humor. I think it is the same for her. We can tell each other anything without fear of being judged. We are psychologically sophisticated enough to realize that what each sees in the other is a composite of our experience, fantasies and inner contrasexual sides. That keeps us within comfortable boundaries. Oh, and she is firmly married; that helps too.

I could write about relationships into the wee hours, as I have in other books,[54] but I can say here, succinctly, that in my experience the unattainable is the most desirable, and once attained, most difficult to let go of. I am almost always in love, or about to fall, but not always with the one who wants me. Unrequited love and frustrated desire are certainly the pits, and I have had my share of them too. Desire acknowledged but

---

[53] Natalie Cole, "Almost Like Being in Love"; Ascap.

[54] See esp. *Getting to Know You: The Inside Out of Relationship*.

deliberately suppressed is something else entirely, and not something Freud gave much credence to, except as a neurotic symptom.

Marriage (or any long-term relationship) is so bizarre with its twists and turns. Love may survive, but desire may die, or vice versa. Relationships are fraught with the unpredictable. Eros is a whimsical god. I am, as is well known, on the side of romance, but there are so many psychological obstacles in the way that I often despair. As well, there can be a gap between love and desire that is not easily bridged. Can you love without desire? Of course, and we experience this all the time in close relationships with whatever gender. And when we are attached, we can still desire someone else. This is the human condition, like it or not.

Typologically, love derives from the feeling function (what the other is worth to you). Desire on the other hand is associated with sensation (the physical senses). Love and desire are not antinomies, but rather complementary. Desire is perhaps the more incendiary experience, but love without desire, while sometimes frustrating for one or both, can still be satisfying, more enduring, and way better than no love at all.

The distance between being in love and simply loving is hard to gauge, but there is certainly a difference. In general, the former is marked by the need to be constantly close to the loved one, while simply loving is much looser about physical propinquity. At least that is my opinion. And when you have two people passionately "in love," you have what is commonly known as a *folie à deux* (two crazy people).

Now, open your heart to jazz-bird Madeleine Peyroux, who with the lyrics of master romancer Leonard Cohen could charm an anchorite off his pole:

> Dance me to your beauty with a burning violin
> Dance me through the panic 'til I'm gathered safely in
> Lift me like an olive branch and be my homeward dove
> Dance me to the end of love
> Dance me to the end of love
>
> Oh let me see your beauty when the witnesses are gone
> Let me feel you moving like they do in Babylon

Show me slowly what I only know the limits of
Dance me to the end of love
Dance me to the end of love

Dance me to the wedding now, dance me on and on
Dance me very tenderly and dance me very long
We're both of us beneath our love, we're both of us above
Dance me to the end of love
Dance me to the end of love

Dance me to the children who are asking to be born
Dance me through the curtains that our kisses have outworn
Raise a tent of shelter now, though every thread is torn
Dance me to the end of love

Dance me to your beauty with a burning violin
Dance me through the panic till I'm gathered safely in
Touch me with your naked hand or touch me with your glove
Dance me to the end of love
Dance me to the end of love.[55]

Well, that is to my mind the quintessential love song. I can't get enough of it. What lover or wannabe could resist those evocative lyrics? What could better express the passion inherent in aloneness? Only Eros can assuage the panic that is endemic in everyday life.

Leonard Cohen is one of my rascally heroes (second only to the libidinous Henry Miller) in the realm of nonsense/Eros, so no wonder the above lyrics and melody drive me up the wall with desire for a warm and willing body. Madeleine Peyroux was only recently known to me, but you can Google her, or see her on YouTube, and know everything about her that I do. I can tell you this much: she has a voice to rip your heart out. I haven't been moved as much since I chanced upon that once little-known British songbird, Corinne Bailey Rae.

I have already acknowledged here that I am rather easily seduced; and given time with a willing body I can also fall in love. This does not make me remarkable among men; rather it underlines my ordinary erotic male-

---

[55] "Dance Me to the End of Love," on *Careless Love* (2004), lyrics by Leonard Cohen; Ascap.

ness, whatever else I may be or do in the realm of Logos or for the larger Jungian community.

I have meanwhile been thinking of how the Pleroma fascinates me, and I don't know why. I somehow had the vague impression that the Pleroma was never-ever land, though I never seriously looked into it until just yesterday.

This may seem off-topic, but this book is, after all, about nonsense, and very little is off that topic.

There is a bewildering lot to ponder when you start focusing on the Pleroma. For a start, is it outer or inner? You can lose many a night's sleep over such a question, as I have in discussing it with my friend Ms. Cotton Pants. The word Pleroma isn't even in the *American Heritage Dictionary*. Wikipedia (which we all know isn't the most reliable authority) has it as "the plurality of divine powers," whatever that means.

There are a number of passing references to the Pleroma in Jung's *Collected Works,* and they are my lodestone, however enigmatic. His comments are not substantial enough to quote here, but in his letters we find a few notable passages:

> For my private use I call the sphere of paradoxical existence, i.e, the instinctive unconscious, the Pleroma, a term borrowed from Gnosticism. The reflection and formation of the Pleroma in the individual consciousness produce an image of it (of like nature in a certain sense), and that is the symbol. In it all paradoxes are abolished. In the Pleroma, Above and Below lie together in a strange way and produce nothing, but when it is disturbed by the mistakes and needs of the individual a waterfall arises between Above and Below, a dynamic something that is the symbol. Like the Pleroma, the symbol is greater than man. It overpowers him, shapes him, as though he had opened a sluice that pours a mighty stream over him and sweeps him away.[56]

There are other minor references in Jung's letters, but I take from them that the Pleroma refers to the vast realm of unconsciousness and/or

---

[56] *C. G.Jung Letters,* vol. 1, p. 61.

the unconscious itself, which is to say, everything we are usually unaware of. We are immersed in it, as fish are in water. Edward F. Edinger writes pithily about that notion:

> The center of transpersonal identity—which we call the Self—needs to be discovered within the psyche of the individual, rather than being projected onto the community [family, tribe, ethnic grouping]. So long as the latter pertains, the community is the carrier of the Self, and individuals—in so far as they are identified with the community—are irresponsible. The image that I like to use is that of a fish swimming in a pond. I often speak of a Zen koan that asks the question, "Who discovered water?" And the answer to the question is, "Not the fish." That particular little story has considerable relevance for psychologists and analysts, you see, because initially we all live like fish swimming around in the unconscious quite blissfully, unaware of the medium that surrounds us. And as long as we're in that state, the science of psychology cannot exist. Who's going to ask what's the nature of water in such a situation? Water would not have been distinguished as a separate entity from one's being. But, if one is a lungfish, then it's one's destiny to get out of the water; because as one starts losing gills and develops lungs, one is about to suffocate in that water. Unless the lungfish climbs out onto dry land and into the atmosphere, it will perish. And when it's out, then the lungfish discovers, "Oh, where I was back there, that's water!" These are the issues that one must engage when confronting our topic.[57]

So, as I see it, we shuffle about in the Pleroma until we get bored or reach the end of our tether, whichever comes first. Then we may be inclined to take stock of our lives—who are we without our workaday and family persona? What do we really want to do? Who do we want to be? Who do we want to be with? Where does our energy want to go? These questions commonly precipitate a crisis in midlife—typically 35-50, but often even years earlier or later. And they can recur throughout life.

The Pleroma is a place of fullness, that is to say, a place of unity, oneness, where there is no differentiation from one's tribe, one's cultural

---

[57] "The Question of a Jungian Community," in George R. Elder and Dianne D. Cordic, eds., *An American Jungian: In Honor of Edward F. Edinger,* pp. 200-201. [First published in *Psychological Perspectives* (vol. 48, no. 1, 2005)]

environment, a swamp of unconsciousness. We call it *participation mystique,* an unconscious identification with the family or a religious group, or indeed an institution. Contrast that now with the concept of *creatura* (Latin, literally creature). *Creatura* is a state of twoness, the world of differentiation, division, conflict, living with the opposites. *Creatura* opens the door to an adventurous dialogue with the unconscious. It is considerably less comfortable than the Pleroma, but potentially more satisfying and meaningful.

You know you've left the tribe when you'd rather be home by yourself than out in the world chasing pussy by speed-dating. I mean this to be a genderless observation.

A few sessions of personal analysis can get you over an immediate Pleromatic hump, but long term you have to keep track of yourself—what irritates you, what sparks your interest, what you dream about, the accidental/synchronistic events that befall you and so on.

*

I got up early this morning and dropped in on CHIROPRACTIC FOR LIFE, a clinic just around the corner. I have passed it hundreds of times over the years without a thought. But just lately I have been suffering with neck spasms and lower back pain, and I was motivated to seek advice.

I was well received by the winsome receptionist Leslie and given an appointment for this very afternoon, at which time Dr. Barbara Smith, DC, examined me, scanned for spinal inflammation and did some adjustments. The neck and lower back pain is relieved already and I will continue with treatments tomorrow and next week and on. And chiropractic is also touted as good for the immune system (helpful news for those of us who eschew the flu vaccine) and an aid in quitting smoking.

Vertebral subluxation is so sexy, don't you think? Dr. Barb uses the KST (Koren Specific Technique) approach, non-invasive and non-violent. No snapping of the head, cracking of bones, etc. Attractive middle-aged blonde, which helps too. I took away and read a lot of flyers explaining it all. Short story: I am hooked on chiropractic, to say nothing of Dr. Barb, once an Ice Capades figure skater, whose skillful touch won

me over immediately.[58] I see a halo/glow around her, which is not unusual when one enters into a new therapeutic relationship.

Well, I'll get over it, or not.

****

Twenty-Five
Bette Davis Eyes

"Solitude is all well and good, but being a solitaire for an extended
period of time is not healthy for the soul."
—Prof. Adam Brillig (ret.)

The above comment refers, I believe, to the narcissistic traps that await
the man or woman who lacks a warm and willing body other than their
own—or, to be more inclusive, those who long for Eros with a mate
whose ego-awareness is not limited to, say, sports and/or business.

There is not much one can say "in general" about such situations, for
each case is unique, depending on the background, complexes and expectations of each of the partners. The more one is invested in the collective
Pleroma of unconsciousness, the worse it is for the individuals.

Back to narcissism; its symptoms are self-absorption, indifference to
the views of others, and a pronounced inclination to trust only one's own
thoughts and feelings. Such an attitude demeans others, drives them
away and leaves you alone again—mean minded, depressed and grumpy.

Of course by then you are so travel-averse and so used to your own
company that you don't have the energy to visit distant friends. Maybe
you Skype and you Twitter, but you're too introverted for Facebook and
Second Life. You don't have the energy to go out dating, so you hang
around taking care of business and wait for someone to fall into your lap.

---

[58] She has a website: www.doctorbarb.com.

110

You know you are loved by friends and relatives, but it doesn't assuage your longing for a companion to share your bed.

A friend wonders: do we blog and twitter because we are in a fog and dither about life? I could agree, but who's to know?

You've pretty much exhausted your intellectual resources. You feel bereft and you toy with the idea of throwing yourself offa bridge. But then you wake up sobbing from a dream something like this:

> I am on a street in the center of a deserted city, surrounded by cavernous buildings. I am bouncing a ball between the buildings, from one to another. It keeps getting away from me; I can't pin it down. I wake up in a cold sweat, terrified, sobbing uncontrollably.

Okay, folks, truth to tell, that was my dream, the one that took me into analysis some fifty years ago. It doesn't sound like much, but it put paid to the life I had been leading. I had a wife and three children, an accomplished persona, but my shadow, or let's say "unlived life," was crippling me. I had lost control of the "ball," metaphorically my wholeness.[59]

What to do? Well, I went into analysis and for the next six months learned more about myself than I ever wanted to know. More, and the hardest consequence: I left the wife and children I loved, suffered through the loss and said Yes to a new life. This is not a path that as a professional analyst I recommend to others; it's just too painful, and few have the heart for it. I got lucky and found my vocation, or rather, I was hurled into it by the powers that be.

I had a benign childhood and adolescence, surrounded by loving friends and relatives. No one could ask for better. But I went off the rails later in life. This puts the lie to Freud's theory that neurosis has its roots in early life. I was culturally and environmentally neurotic. I bought into the North American ethic: consumerism, ambition, productivity. I did all the "right" things but I had no idea who I really was. I think I am less neurotic now, but happy?—no, that word isn't in my lexicon. Life is in-

---

[59] This motif forms the substance of my book, *Not the Big Sleep: On Having Fun Seriously*, which subsequently developed into the **SleepNot Trilogy**, together with *On Staying Awake: Getting Older and Bolder*, and *Eyes Wide Open: Late Thoughts*.

finitely more complicated as you become conscious. I am content with myself, but that's as far as I'd go. I talk to my inner Rachel from time to time, and work on dreams with other lost souls. I publish books and write nonsense. These activities keep me in the here and now and relatively sane, though I wouldn't betcher bottom dollar on either. . .

Time to close with another poignant ditty by the young master Cat:

> I'm looking for a hard headed woman,
> One who will take me for myself,
> And if I find my hard headed woman,
> I won't need nobody else, no, no, no.
> I'm looking for a hard headed woman,
> One who will make me do my best,
> And if I find my hard headed woman
> I know the rest of my life will be blessed—yes, yes, yes.
> I know a lot of fancy dancers,
> People who can glide you on a floor,
> They move so smooth but have no answers.
> When you ask why'd you come here for?
> I don't know why?
> I know many fine feathered friends
> But their friendliness depends on how you do.
> They know many sure fired ways
> To find out the one who pays
> And how you do.
> I'm looking for a hard headed woman,
> One who will make me feel so good,
> And if I find my hard headed woman,
> I know my life will be as it should—yes, yes, yes.
> I'm looking for a hard headed woman,
> One who will make me do my best,
> And if I find my hard headed woman....[60]

Of course, there is more to this than meets the eye. There always is; e.g. a hard headed woman may be more than I could cope with...

---

[60] Cat Stevens, "Hard Headed Woman," from *Tea for the Tillerman;* Ascap.

****

Twenty-Six
Tea for Three

If you ever promised yourself that one day you would read Marcel Proust's prodigious tomes, *In Search of Lost Time* (1913+), you can save yourself that chore by reading Alain de Botton's enchanting book of essays entitled *How Proust Can Change Your Life: Not a Novel.* It is absolutely the most delightful book I have read in years. It sits on my shelf next to John O'Donahue's *Anam Cara* and *W.O.W.:Writers on Writing.*

I have labored through Proust's dense and indigestible prose, and I can tell you it isn't worth the effort. If you like Dickens, you will despair reading Proust. There is no plot and nothing ever happens. Proust composed the many volumes over fourteen years under a blanket without an adequate bedside lamp. They are so minutely detail oriented that you want to throw up. It is more depressing even than Joyce's *Ulysses.*[61] You feel stuck forever in the mind of a misanthropic, misogynous, narcissistic creep. You might better play Scrabble with your paramour, or lacking one-such, so-called self-abuse would be time less wasted.

What de Botton does in his little book is beyond remarkable. He not only entices you to read Proust, but makes it unnecessary by eviscerating what has come to be known as the "Proustian temperament," which has its apogee in absolute, unrestrained lethargy—a prime symptom of what we nowadays call puer psychology. *In Search of Lost Time* is essentially literary nonsense writ large.

No wonder Evelyn Waugh said, "I was reading Proust for the first time. Very poor stuff. I think he was mentally defective."[62]

De Botton does his undercover hatchet job by selecting sentences or

---

[61] Se my commentary in *Jung Uncorked,* Book Two, pp. 65ff.

[62] Winokur, *Writers on Writing,* p. 72.

passages from Proust's work and dancing around them with a wily intellect and a feeling function so nuanced as to command respect from the most cynical reader.

It would be foolish of me to try to paraphrase de Botton's laconic riffs on Proust's prose and life, but I can tell you I was bowled over reading chapters entitled "How to Love Life Today" through "How to Express Your Emotions" to "How To Be Happy in Love."

I highly commend this gem to all who wish to know themselves a little better—by reading de Botton, not Proust.

*

I am going to leave you soon, but you can bet your bottom dollar that I will start a new book before long, I am not famous, but I am prolific. I wouldn't know what to do with myself otherwise.

In the meantime, here's a song from the incomparable Ms. Streisand's latest album, *Barbra: Love Is the Answer:*

> No complaints and no regrets
> I still believe in chasing dreams and placing bets
> But I have learned that all you give is all you get,
> So give it all you got.
>
> I had my share, Idrank my fill and even
> Though I'm satisfied I'm hungry still
> To see what's down another road beyond
> A hill and do it all again.
>
> So here's to life and all the joy it brings.
> Here's to life, the dreamers and their dreams.
> Funnyhow the time just flies.
> How love can turn from warm hellos to sad goodbyes
> And leave you with the memories you're memorized
> To keep your winters warm.
>
> There's no yes in yesterday,
> And who knows what tomorrow brings or takes away.
> As long as I'm still in the game I want to play
> For laughs, for life, for love.

So here's to life and all the joy it brings.
Here's to life the dreamers and their dreams.
May all your storms be weathered
And all that's good get better.
Here's to life, here's to love, here's to you.[63]

'Nuff said.

Finis

---

[63] "Here's to Life," lyrics by Artie Butler and Phyllis Molinary; Ascap.

Bibliography

Arnold, Matthew. "On Dover Beach." In *Norton Anthology of Poetry*. 3rd ed. Ed. A. W. Allison et al. New York: W. W. Norton & Company, 1970.

Carotenuto, Aldo. *Eros and Pathos: Shades of Love and Suffering*. Toronto: Inner City Books, 1989.

Carr, Allen. *Allen Carr's Easy Way to Stop Smoking*. Canadian ed. Oakville, Ontario: Clarity Publishing, 2004.

Colombo, John Robert. *Colombo's All-Time Great Canadian Quotations*. Toronto: Stoddart, 1994.

De Botton, Alain: *How Proust Can Change Your Life: Not a Novel*. New York: Pantheon Books, 1997.

Edinger, Edward F. *Anatomy of the Psyche: Alchemical Symbolism in Psychotherapy*. La Salle, IL: Open Court, 1985.

_____. *The Creation of Consciousness: Jung's Myth for Modern Man*. Toronto: Inner City Books, 1984.

_____. "M. Esther Harding, 1888-1971." In *Spring 1972*. Zurich: Spring Publications, 1972.

_____. *The Mysterium Lectures: A Journey Through Jung's* Mysterium Coniunctionis. Toronto: Inner City Books, 1995.

_____. *The Mystery of the Coniunctio: Alchemical Image of Individuation*. Toronto: Inner City Books, 1994.

_____. *Science of the Soul: A Jungian Perspective*. Toronto: Inner City Books, 2002.

Elder, George R., and Cordic, Dianne D., eds. *An American Jungian: In Honor of Edward F. Edinger*. Toronto: Inner City Books, 2009.

Freud, Sigmund. *New Introductory Lectures on Psycho-Analysis* (1933), lecture 21. In *The Complete Psychological Works of Sigmund Freud*. Ed. James Strachey. London, UK: The Hogarth Press, 1978.

Frey-Rohn, Liliane. *From Freud to Jung: A Comparative Study of the Psychology of the Unconscious*. Boston: Shambhala Publications, 1974.

Frost, Robert. "The Road Not Taken." In *Mountain Interval*. New York: Henry Holt and Company, 1920.

Grimm Brothers. *The Complete Grimm's Fairy Tales*. New York: Pantheon Books, 1944.

Hall, James A., and Sharp, Daryl, eds. *Marie-Louise von Franz: The Classic Jungian and the Classic Jungian Tradition*. Toronto: Inner City Books, 2008.

Hannah, Barbara. *Jung: His Life and Work (A Biographical Memoir)*. New York: Capricorn Books, G.P. Putnam's Sons, 1976.

Hollis, James. *The Middle Passage: From Misery to Meaning in Midlife*. Toronto: Inner City Books, 1993.

_____. *The Eden Project: In Search of the Magical Other*. Toronto: Inner City Books, 1998.

_____. *Under Saturn's Shadow: The Wounding and Healing of Men*. Toronto: Inner City Books, 1994.

Jacoby, Mario. *The Analytic Encounter: Transference and Human Relationship*. Toronto: Inner City Books, 1984.

_____. *Longing for Paradise: Psychological Perspectives on an Archetype*. Toronto: Inner City Books, 2006.

Jones, Rick, and Neale, Valerie. *Life Drawing*. CD; Ascap; © Half a Brain Music, 2009; www.RicknVal.com.

Jung, C. G. *C. G. Jung Letters*. (Bollingen Series XCV). 2 vols. Ed. G. Adler and A. Jaffé. Princeton: Princeton University Press, 1973.

_____. *The Collected Works of C. G. Jung* (Bollingen Series XX). 20 vols. Trans. R. F. C. Hull. Ed. H. Read, M. Fordham, G. Adler, Wm. McGuire. Princeton: Princeton University Press, 1953-1979.

_____. *Memories, Dreams, Reflections*. Ed. Aniela Jaffé. New York: Pantheon Books, 1961.

_____. *Visions: Notes of the Seminar Given in 1930-1934* (Bollingen Series XCIX). 2 vols. Ed. Claire Douglas. Princeton: Princeton University Press, 1997.

Jung, Carl G., and von Franz, Marie-Louise, eds. *Man and His Symbols*. London, UK: Aldus Books, 1964.

Kaufmann, Walter, ed. and trans. *The Portable Nietzsche*. New York: Viking Press, 1954.

Kreinheder, Albert. *Body and Soul: The Other Side of Illness*. 2nd edition. Toronto: Inner City Books, 2008.

Leacock, Stephen. *Sunshine Sketches of a Little Town*. In *The Penguin Stephen Leacock*. New York: Penguin, 1981.

Lightman, Allan. *Einstein's Dreams: A Novel*. New York: Warner Books, 1994; Vintage Books, 2004.

Malcolm, Janet. *Psychoanalysis: The Impossible Profession*. New York: Alfred A. Knopf, 1981.

Mansfield, Sue. *The Gestalts of War: An inquiry into its origins and meanings as a social institution*. New York: Dial Press, 1982.

McGuire, William, ed. *The Freud/Jung Letters* (Bollingen Series XCIV). Trans. Ralph Manheim and R. F. C. Hull. Princeton: Princeton University Press, 1974.

McGuire, William, and Hull, R. F. C., eds. *C. G. Jung Speaking: Interviews and Encounters* (Bollingen Series XCVII. Princeton: Princeton University Press, 1977.

Meredith, Margaret Eileen. *The Secret Garden: Temenos for Individuation*. Toronto: Inner City Books, 2005.

Monick, Eugene. *Phallos: Sacred Image of the Masculine*. Toronto: Inner City Books, 1987.

O'Donahue, John. *Anam Cara: A Book of Celtic Wisdom*. New York: Harper-Collins, 1997.

Onians, R.B. *The Origins of European Thought*. Cambridge, MA: Cambridge University Press, 1951.

Perera, Sylvia Brinton. *Descent to the Goddess: A Way of Initiation for Women*. Toronto: Inner City Books, 1981.

Pethick, Jerry. *On Holography and a Way to Make Holograms*. Burlington, ON: Belltower Enterprises, 1971; Toronto: Inner City Books, 2010.

Qualls-Corbett, Nancy. *The Sacred Prostitute: Eternal Aspect of the Feminine*. Toronto: Inner City Books, 1988.

Rank, Otto. *The Trauma of Birth*. New York: Brunner, 1952.

118

Rilke, Rainer Maria. *The Notebook of Malte Laurids Brigge.* Trans. John Linton. London, UK: The Hogarth Press, 1959.

_____. *Rilke on Love and Other Difficulties.* Ed. John Mood. New York, Norton, 1975.

_____. *Rainer Maria Rilke, Sonnets to Orpheus.* Trans. Willis Barnstone. Boston, MA: Shambhala, 2004.

Sharp, Daryl. *Chicken Little: The Inside Story (a Jungian romance).* Toronto: Inner City Books, 1993.

_____. *Dear Gladys: The Survival Papers, Book. 2.* Toronto: Inner City Books, 1989.

_____. *Digesting Jung: Food for the Journey.* Toronto: Inner City Books, 2001.

_____. *Eyes Wide Open: Late Thoughts (a Jungian romance).* Toronto: Inner City Books, 2007.

_____. *Getting To Know You: The Inside Out of Relationship.* Toronto: Inner City Books, 1992.

_____. *Jung Lexicon: A Primer of Terms and Concepts.* Toronto: Inner City Books, 1991.

_____. *Jung Uncorked: Rare Vintages from the Cellar of Analytical Psychology.* 4 vols. Toronto: Inner City Books, 2008-9.

_____. *Jungian Psychology Unplugged: My Life as an Elephant.* Toronto, Inner City Books, 1998.

_____. *Living Jung: The Good and the Better.* Toronto: Inner City Books, 1996.

_____. *Not the Big Sleep: On Having Fun, Seriously (a Jungian romance).* Toronto: Inner City Books, 2005.

_____. *On Staying Awake: Getting Older and Bolder (another Jungian romance).* Toronto: Inner City Books, 2006.

_____. *Personality Types: Jung's Model of Typology.* Toronto: Inner City Books, 1987.

_____. *The Secret Raven: Conflict and Transformation in the Life of Franz Kafka.* Toronto: Inner City Books, 1980.

119

_____. *The Survival Papers: Anatomy of a Midlife Crisis.* Toronto: Inner City Books, 1988.

_____. *Who Am I, Really? Personality, Soul and Individuation.* Toronto: Inner City Books, 1995.

Sparks, J. Gary. *At the Heart of Matter: Synchronicity and Jung's Spiritual Testament.* Toronto: Inner City Books, 2007.

Stevens, Anthony. *Archetype Revisited: An Updated Natural History of the Self.* Toronto: Inner City Books, 2003.

Storr, Anthony. *Solitude.* London, UK: HarperCollins Publishers, 1997.

Von Franz, Marie-Louise. *Alchemy: An Introduction to the Symbolism and the Psychology.* Toronto: Inner City Books, 1980.

_____. *Animus and Anima in Fairy Tales.* Toronto: Inner City Books, 2002.

_____. *C. G. Jung: His Myth in Our Time.* Toronto: Inner City Books, 1998.

_____. *On Divination and Synchronicity.* Toronto: Inner City Books, 1980.

_____. *On Dreams and Death: A Jungian Interpretation.* Foreword by Emmanuel Kennedy-Xipolitas, Trans. Emmanuel Kennedy-Xipolitas and Vernon Brooks. Chicago, IL: Open Court, 1998.

_____. *The Problem of the Puer Aeternus.* Revised edition. Ed. Daryl Sharp. Toronto: Inner City Books, 2000.

_____. *Projection and Re-Collection in Jungian Psychology: Reflections of the Soul.* Trans. William H. Kennedy. La Salle, IL: Open Court, 1980.

_____. *A Psychological Interpretation of the Golden Ass of Apuleius: The Liberation of the Feminine in Man.* Revised ed. Boston: Shambhala Publications, 1992.

_____. *Redemption Motifs in Fairy Tales.* Toronto: Inner City Books, 1980.

Von Franz, Marie-Louise, and Hillman, James. *Jung's Typology.* New York: Spring Publications, 1971.

Wilhelm, Richard, trans. *The I Ching or Book of Changes.* Rendered into English by Cary F. Baynes. London, UK: Routledge & Kegan Paul, 1968.

Winokur, Jon. *W.O.W.: Writers on Writing.* Philadelphia, PA: Running Press, 1990.

Index

Also in this Series by Daryl Sharp

Please see next page for discounts and postage/handling.

THE SECRET RAVEN: Conflict and Transformation in the Life of Franz Kafka
ISBN 978-0-919123-00-7. (1980) 128 pp. $25

PERSONALITY TYPES: Jung's Model of Typology
ISBN 978-0-919123-30-9. (1987) 128 pp. Diagrams $25

THE SURVIVAL PAPERS: Anatomy of a Midlife Crisis
ISBN 978-0-919123-34-2. (1988) 160 pp. $25

DEAR GLADYS: The Survival Papers, Book 2
ISBN 978-0-919123-36-6. (1989) 144 pp. $25

JUNG LEXICON: A Primer of Terms and Concepts
ISBN 978-0-919123-48-9. (1991) 160 pp. Diagrams $25

GETTING TO KNOW YOU: The Inside Out of Relationship
ISBN 978-0-919123-56-4. (1992) 128 pp. $25

THE BRILLIG TRILOGY:

    1. CHICKEN LITTLE: The Inside Story *(A Jungian romance)*
    ISBN 978-0-919123-62-5. (1993) 128 pp. $25

    2. WHO AM I, REALLY? Personality, Soul and Individuation
    ISBN 978-0-919123-68-7. (1995) 144 pp. $25

    3. LIVING JUNG: The Good and the Better
    ISBN 978-0-919123-73-1. (1996) 128 pp. $25

JUNGIAN PSYCHOLOGY UNPLUGGED: My Life as an Elephant
ISBN 978-0-919123-81-6. (1998) 160 pp. $25

DIGESTING JUNG: Food for the Journey
ISBN 978-0-919123-96-0. (2001) 128 pp. $25

JUNG UNCORKED: Rare Vintages from the Cellar of Analytical Psychology
Four books. ISBN 978-1-894574-21-1/22-8/24-2/27-3 (2008-9) 128 pp. each. $25 each

THE SLEEPNOT TRILOGY:

    1. NOT THE BIG SLEEP: On having fun, seriously *(A Jungian romance)*
    ISBN 978-0-894574-13-6. (2005) 128 pp. $25

    2. ON STAYING AWAKE: Getting Older and Bolder *(Another Jungian romance)*
    ISBN 978-0-894574-16-7. (2006) 144 pp. $25

    3. EYES WIDE OPEN: Late Thoughts *(Another Jungian romance)*
    ISBN 978-0-894574-18-1. (2007) 160 pp. $25

Studies in Jungian Psychology
by Jungian Analysts *Quality Paperbacks*

Prices and payment in $US (except in Canada, and Visa orders, $Cdn)

Jung and Yoga: The Psyche-Body Connection
Judith Harris (London, Ontario) ISBN 978-0-919123-95-3. 160 pp. $25

The Gambler: Romancing Lady Luck
Billye B. Currie (Jackson, MS) 978-1-894574-19-8. 128 pp. $25

Conscious Femininity: Interviews with Marion Woodman
Introduction by Marion Woodman (Toronto) ISBN 978-0-919123-59-5. 160 pp. $25

The Sacred Psyche: A Psychological Approach to the Psalms
Edward F. Edinger (Los Angeles) ISBN 978-1-894574-09-9. 160 pp. $25

Eros and Pathos: Shades of Love and Suffering
Aldo Carotenuto (Rome) ISBN 978- 0-919123-39-7. 144 pp. $25

Descent to the Goddess: A Way of Initiation for Women
Sylvia Brinton Perera (New York) ISBN 978-0-919123-05-2. 112 pp. $25

Addiction to Perfection: The Still Unravished Bride
Marion Woodman (Toronto) ISBNj 978-0-919123-11-3. Illustrated. 208 pp. $30/$35hc

The Illness That We Are: A Jungian Critique of Christianity
John P. Dourley (Ottawa) ISBN 978-0-919123-16-8. 128 pp. $25

Coming To Age: The Croning Years and Late-Life Transformation
Jane R. Prétat (Providence) ISBN 978-0-919123-63-2. 144 pp. $25

Jungian Dream Interpretation: A Handbook of Theory and Practice
James A. Hall, M.D. (Dallas) ISBN 978-0-919123-12-0. 128 pp. $25

Phallos: Sacred Image of the Masculine
Eugene Monick (Scranton) ISBN 978-0-919123-26-7. 30 illustrations. 144 pp. $25

The Sacred Prostitute: Eternal Aspect of the Feminine
Nancy Qualls-Corbett (Birmingham) ISBN 978-0-919123-31-1. Illus. 176 pp. $30

Longing for Paradise: Psychological Perspectives on an Archetype
Mario Jacoby (Zurich) ISBN 978-1-894574-17-4. 240 pp. $35

The Pregnant Virgin: A Process of Psychological Development
Marion Woodman (Toronto) ISBN 978-0-919123-20-5. Illus. 208 pp. $30pb/$35hc

Discounts: any 3-5 books, 10%; 6-9 books, 20%; 10-19, 25%; 20 or more, 40% .

Add Postage/Handling: 1-2 books, $6 surface ($10 air); 3-4 books, $8 surface

($12 air); 5-9 books, $15 surface ($20 air); 10 or more, $15 surface ($30 air)

Visa credit cards accepted. Toll-free: Tel. 1-888-927-0355; Fax 1-888=924-1814.

INNER CITY BOOKS, Box 1271, Station Q, Toronto, ON M4T 2P4, Canada
Tel. (416) 927-0355 / Fax (416) 924-1814 / booksales@innercitybooks.net